4.00

No 3 Putts

What the Pros Really Want You to Know to Improve Your Putting

David Perry

WISE
MEDIA GROUP

Copyright © 2012 by David Perry
No 3 Putts: What the Pros Really Want You to Know to Improve Your Putting
http://no3putts.50interviews.com

ISBN: 978-1-935689-54-6

Published by Wise Media Group
Colorado, USA
www.WiseMediaGroup.com

All rights reserved. No part of this book may be reproduced in any form or by any electronic or mechanical means, including information storage and retrieval systems, without written permission from the author, except in the case of a reviewer, who may quote brief passages embodied in critical articles or in a review.

Trademarked names appear throughout this book. Rather than use a trademark symbol with every occurrence of a trademarked name, names are used in an editorial fashion, with no intention of infringement of the respective owner's trademark.

The information in this book is distributed on an "as is" basis, without warranty. Although every precaution has been taken in the preparation of this work, neither the author nor the publisher shall have any liability to any person or entity with respect to any loss or damage caused or alleged to be caused directly or indirectly by the information contained in this book.

The resources listed in this book are the recommendations and resources of the interviewees and are not necessarily recommendations of the author or 50 Interviews.

Original 50 Interviews concept by Brian Schwartz
Cover Design by Patryk Sobczak
Digital Layout by KindleExpert.com
Print Layout by Veronica Yager

This book is dedicated to all golfers who make the game what it is today, drawing in millions of players and fans around the world. My desire is to have all golfers improve their putting skills to lower their score and have more fun with friends, both old and new.

To my mother and father who introduced me to the wonderful world of golf.

Dave "No 3 Putts" Perry

Table of Contents

Foreword i

Chris Foley
    Director of Chris Foley Golf School 1

John Hughes
    Executive Vice President/
    National Director of Instruction at
    Advantage Golf School 7

Shim Lagoy
    Orinda CC Master PGA Professional 27

Becky Dengler
    LPGA Master Golf Teaching Professional 39

Carol Preisinger
    Golf Magazine Top 100 Teacher in America,
    2005-Present 51

Dan Schwabe
    Northern California PGA Teacher of the Year 65

Mike Shannon
    One of America's Top 50 Greatest
    Teachers (Golf Digest) 75

Andy Thompson
    Golf Digest Top 100 Fitter 85

Mardell Wilkins
  Top 50 Best Teacher, Golf Digest and LPGA 95

Sam Emerson
  PGA Horton Smith Award Winner for
  Instructor and Club Fitter 103

About the Author 113

Acknowledgements 115

Foreword

Every score in golf ends on the putting green, but this is where players spend the least amount of time developing skill. Compared to the rest of the game, putting is a relatively easy task, but few people ever get consistently good at it. They spend five minutes before each round putting a few balls on the practice green, then run to the first tee. Meanwhile they have learned nothing about putting skills and probably nothing that will actually help them during their round—other than getting a feel for the green speed. Even tour players who spend hours and hours on the putting green don't putt at the level they want, because simply racking up hours is an inefficient way to learn without structured skill development. So what are those skills? At a high level putting requires that you read the green correctly and then start the ball on your intended line with the correct speed. Sounds simple, but each component needs to be understood and practiced with correct feedback.

It all starts with good green reading, which is the process of correctly predicting the effect of gravity, slope, and time on your putt so that you can choose the correct target, as well as understand how hard to hit the ball. Next comes alignment, stroke, and pace—the ability to hit the ball on your target line with the correct speed. Surprisingly, green reading has not been taught in the past. Even more surprisingly, only 2% of all golfers can aim their putters and start their ball on the intended line, including tour players, but few people even realize it.

If you don't know your errors, how can you fix them? This book is about acquiring the skills you need to be a great putter. The encouraging news is that anyone can become better at putting. Putting doesn't require any special strength, flexibility, or decades of experience. It just requires that you know what skills you need and systematically strive to improve them. Each of the skills is relatively simple, so let's get to it...

Mark Sweeney
CEO - AimPoint Technologies
www.aimpointgolf.com

Chris Foley
Director of Chris Foley Golf School

"If you can play with a quiet mind, you are going to play great golf."

Chris Foley's golf instruction methods are based on helping the golfer learn why their golf ball is going where it is, and ultimately diagnosing and correcting their own swing. His approach is aided by extensive use of state of the art, computerized video equipment. Chris has been teaching golf for 21 years and averages over 1,000 students per year.

- PGA Master Professional
- 2002 Minnesota PGA Teacher of the Year

www.chrisfoleygolf.com

There are millions of new and high handicapped golfers playing every year. How do these golfers need to view the importance of putting in their game?
In relationship to score, it's one of the most important parts of the game. Everybody tends to spend a lot of time

on the full swing as a new player. If they were to spend an equal amount of time or split their time between the full swing and putting the short game, I think they would shoot much better scores, much more rapidly.

The putt can be the most important, most frustrating, most misunderstood and least practiced shot in golf. What are the key things about the putt that every golfer needs to fully understand to build a base for accurate, consistent, and enjoyable putting?
The most important part of putting is distance control and learning how to hit the putt at the correct speed. The second most important thing is the ability to aim the putter correctly. If you don't aim the putter correctly, the rest of the stroke is compensation or a series of compensations. Third would be the mechanics of making a good stroke.

> *"...they just don't spend enough time practicing."*

Do you feel people overlook the key elements of a good putt?
One of the things that separates a very good player from an average player or a higher handicapped player, is that ability to control distance on the putting green. People, especially average and higher handicapped players, think of it in terms of speed control.

You hear about golfers throwing and breaking putters over missed putts. What are the biggest mistakes you see golfers make that limit their putting ability?
The ability to gauge distance and speed and the ability to read the green—an awareness of how the putt is going to break.

In your experience what are the road blocks that prevent golfers from becoming good putters?

If you don't aim the putter properly, you build a stroke around that and when we test people, only about 1 in 10 people can aim the putter to the center of the cup on an 8-or-10-foot putt. So if you can't aim the putter correctly, it's hard to create the consistent stroke; you are building compensations in your stroke to be able to hit the golf ball on the line.

> *"Good putters believe they are good putters."*

It starts with their lack of aiming skill. Then as far as road blocks go, they just don't spend enough time practicing. Putting tends to be boring; it's a lot more fun to drive the ball 200, 250 yards than it is to hit a six foot putt. To be a good putter you have to enjoy practicing it. To do that you have to create games and drills and things that make putting less boring.

Every weekend we see professionals miss simple putts. Why? What is going on that makes them miss these seemingly easy putts?
When it gets to that level, the players we are seeing on TV, it's one of a couple things: it's either a miss-read or its tension and poor thinking. Where there's enough on the line that they have excess tension, they visualize poorly, and when you visualize poorly it's hard to hit the correct putt.

What are the characteristics and attitudes that make a great putter?
Anything we do in the game of golf, we need to do it with a clear mind. Good putters believe they are good putters. There's a lot to that. The best putters tend to have the best mechanics, the ability to aim the putter square and the ability to make a consistent stroke that returns the putter to square each time, and deliver with the correct speed.

If you had to pick one golfer as a role model for putting, who would it be and what would make them a good role model?
That's such a hard question because there are so many great putters. I love Steve Stricker's putting stroke and the way he moves around on the greens. The best putters of all time are Greg Norman and Tiger Woods. If you look at those three guys, they are pretty hard to beat.

Putts within 10 feet are the most stressful. How should golfers approach this situation especially to avoid the dreaded 3 putt?
It goes back to distance control, like we talked about earlier. The speed that you are going to hit the putt influences how you read the green. If you have the ability to hit every putt 6-to-12-inches past the hole, that is the perfect speed to make putts. That's where the putt for the hole is the largest in size. So if you have good distance control and then the ability to read the break, and then have good mechanics, you are going to be very successful with those 10 footers.

What do you need to do to be a good putter? Are there any tips, techniques, or tricks, that have really helped you, your students, or the pros?
Your practice habits are essential. Number one, you have to be able to have a stroke that allows you to make straight putts. If you are going to break your putting practice down into a couple of areas, the first would be working on your stroke and practicing straight putts from three to six feet. Make a lot of repetitions and build confidence by hitting those straight putts, and gauging yourself on whether it's 10 in a row, or 25 in a row, or 50 in a row.

Then I think the second component would be working on exercises that help you with your distance control. One of my favorite drills is to have somebody hit putts from say 6, 12, 18, 24, and 30 feet and having a zone they have to land the ball into — like a box that is three feet by two feet behind the hole. They have to get every putt in that box in order to advance in the drill. Each time you are hitting a different length putt you have to concentrate on the distance.

Finally, you should do some type of exercise where you are working on breaking putts. There's a drill we call a tornado drill. In this drill, you put up to eight balls around the hole at three feet away from the center. You have putts from every angle. After putting those, you then move back to six feet on the same lines and try to make those putts. I think if you practice in those three areas, you are covering all the different aspects of putting. That's going to make you a better putter.

A low score in golf depends on a variety of clubs, skills, and shots. What do you recommend to balance putting in conjunction with these other demands during a round of golf, such as after good shots, after bad shots, or being in a rut?
The best players are playing with a quiet mind, play one shot at a time, and are not looking forward in the game. You can't change any shots that you have already hit. They are in the past, so you have to be able to move on and focus on the next shot.

What are the realistic expectations of putts per hole, putts per round, and other measures that golfers need to measure as they develop their skills?
I like to use what I call "putt-par." The way putt-par works is based on how many greens you hit in regulation. For instance, if you hit 10 greens in regulation on a round, you get 2 putts per green in regulation. Then you get 1 putt for all the other holes. So if you hit 10 greens, your putt-par would be 28. Then you can gauge yourself on how well you putted in relationship to that 28. If you are not hitting

any greens, then in theory you should have a lot fewer putts than if you are hitting a lot of greens in regulation.

Looking back is there anything about putting and golf you wish you had done differently? What do you know now that you wish you had known sooner?
Number one, I would like to have known that ball position influences aim, and by changing your ball position you can fix aim. Secondly, the knowledge of whether you should aim and visualize straight lines or curved lines, either being linear or non-linear. There's a test that we use to determine if someone is a linear or non-linear putter. When you determine this, it frees you up and you don't create conflict in your head by trying to aim or visualize in a way differently than you should be.

Could you elaborate on your first comment a little more — the location of the ball?
Where you place the golf ball in relationship to your feet. For a right handed player, a ball position to the left would be a forward ball position, while a ball position more towards the right foot would be a back ball position.

What would you hope golfers would take away from this interview?
My goal, whether it's doing the interview or writing an article or teaching somebody is that they enjoy the game more. Golf is a game and games were meant to be fun. The more fun we have, the more we are going to play and the better our quality of life is if we enjoy it.

Is there anything else that you would like to share? Anything you think may help or that I have left out or not covered that you think might need to be included?
No, I think you covered a lot of ground here.

John Hughes
Executive Vice President/ National Director of Instruction at Advantage Golf School

"It's ultimately what you do with a putter that is going to determine your success."

John is a PGA Master Professional responsible for the operation and profitability of 21 national locations and its hotel partners, as well as the on-going training and support of 60+ independent contract instructors. John also currently serves the PGA of America on its National Instruction Committee. He has written numerous instruction articles for regional and national publications, as well as serving as a featured presenter at many seminars held around the country.

- Executive Vice President/National Director of Instruction at Advantage Golf School
- Instructor at IJGA/Golf Academy of Hilton Head Island
- National Director of Instruction for Golf Digest Schools
- 2009 North Florida PGA Section Teacher of the Year

- 2011 North Florida PGA Section Horton Smith Award
- Owner at Golf Academy of South Carolina

www.advantagegolfschool.com

There are millions of new and high handicapped golfers playing every year. How do these golfers need to view the importance of putting in their game?
It's the shot that puts the ball in the hole. As romantic as hitting a long drive or hitting a crisp shot can be, it's ultimately what you do with a putter that is going to determine your success. I don't think there is really any other way of describing it. There's so much that people love about this game based on how far they can hit it, but at the end of the day, mathematically, your score is more determined by your putting stroke than the driver.

The putt can be the most important, most frustrating, most misunderstood and least practiced shot in golf. What are the key things about the putt that every golfer needs to fully understand to build a base for accurate, consistent, and enjoyable putting?
For a beginner, there are two major things to pay attention to. First, the centeredness of contact, meaning you are hitting the sweet spot of the putter. People tend to negate that there is a sweet spot to the putter, yet when you hit off-centered putts it can greatly influence where that putt ultimately ends up. The second biggest thing is distance control. Everybody as a beginner, should understand that distance is going to determine and dictate all the other aspects and variables of the putt. Without centeredness of contact, you

> *"...it's ultimately what you do with a putter that is going to determine your success."*

can never have consistency of length or distance. So, the two go hand-in-hand. In our schools, that is truly what we try to focus on the most with beginners. Obviously, as your skill increases, we start talking about other determining factors and variables, but the two main ingredients; can you hit that sweet spot of the putter time in and time out, and can you control your distance time in and time out. Once someone can gain those two consistency factors, they will see more consistency in their putting.

You hear about golfers throwing and breaking putters over missed putts. What are the biggest mistakes you see golfers make that limit their putting ability?
Going back to what I just stated, centeredness of contact and distance control are the two biggest faults or mistakes that I see people make that limit their abilities. The best example I can give you is physics and the forces of nature. One being gravity and the other being propulsion or thrust. The amount of break of a putt is going to be determined not only by gravity influences, but where gravity influences the putt and that's where distance comes into place. It's not so much green reading—you can't read a green until you actually understand how hard you are hitting a putt consistently—whether you are a lay-up type putter, hitting it soft, or you like landing it in the back of the cup.

> *"...distance is going to determine and dictate all the other aspects and variables of the putt."*

Again, it goes back to, "Can I hit it square every time?" As long as those two things are consistent, you can limit the mistakes. In the laws of physics, for every action there is an equal and opposite reaction, so you will always come back to those two items. What it all boils down to is what you are doing prior to a putt to ensure you hit it consistently in the sweet spot, and that you are controlling the distance.

In your experience, what are the road blocks that prevent golfers from becoming good putters?
Commitment would be the first one. Understanding the importance of putting would be second, and willingness to incorporate putting as a regular practice habit would be third. When most people go to the range, they get the 75-count ball bucket and they pound, pound, pound drives. Then they get in their car and go home, or go get a sandwich and a drink. They bypass the putting green, so there is no commitment to it. You really can't get a commitment until you start understanding how putts influence your game numerically. When you understand that, you are probably going to be more willing to dedicate, at the very least, 10 minutes out of every half hour practice session to understanding and developing the basics of good putting within your normal practice habits. This in turn will carry on to the golf course. Until you have the commitment, until you have the knowledge that you are willing to do something, most people are going to completely bypass its importance.

Another road block is failing to put the real value of putting into perspective. I will give you an example: when someone comes to our golf schools, they see a den caddy—a small golf bag—full of golf balls. Den caddies can hold about 325 balls. They will ask, "Are you going to make me hit all those balls?" We then proceed to present them with a mathematical equation that will provide them their answer. Most people who attend a golf school are the typical, average golfer. USGA statistics state the average score for a male is about 98 to 99 and they are going to putt 40 times. Based on those stats, our answer to the person is, "Here are 325 balls. If you hit every ball, how many rounds of golf will you play by doing so?" Using the USGA stats and doing some quick math, hitting 325+ golf balls in one practice session is the equivalent of playing 5+ rounds of golf, not including the 40+ putts per round. When you put numbers into perspective of true value based on total shots executed in a round, reality will start to hit home.

Golfers really need that understanding.
And a good teacher is going to take those numbers and present them in many different ways for that student to understand. Not understanding the real numeric value of putting is in all likelihood the biggest road block. Second is not practicing it enough.

Every weekend we see professionals miss simple putts. Why? What is going on that makes them miss these seemingly easy putts?
The first one is pressure. We all experience pressure that is relative to our life experience. For example: if you are an 18 handicap and you are playing with your best friend, and their ball is in their pocket and you're on the 18th hole with a three footer and your partner looks at you and says, "Hey, it's all up to you Dave," you are going to put a certain quantitative amount of pressure on yourself. That pressure, believe it or not, is identical to the same pressure a tour player is going to experience when facing the same three-foot putt to win a major, or to win their first tour event, or to qualify for the tour. Pressure and the amount of pressure you place upon yourself, are relative to your life engagement and the experiences you create for yourself on the golf course. It's also relevant to the pressure you handle off the golf course. If you don't handle pressure well off the golf course, you really can't expect yourself to handle that kind of pressure on the golf course. When you see a pro missing a putt, there's some implied pressure—whether it's self-implied or implied by peers, family, friends, business interests, or any other outside distraction.

Rick Jensen's book, *Easier Said Than Done*, makes an extremely valid point: You have to ask yourself, "Are you good enough to choke?" In most cases the answer is, "No,

I am not good enough," whether you are a tour pro or whether you are that weekend guy playing a $2 Nassau. The second reason why we see tour players miss short putts is because they have obviously not put themselves in these positions to make this putt under pressure. If you have a fundamental flaw of your core of habits—whether it's your setup, your swing, your ball position, how you read the green; pressure will identify and exacerbate the flaw. Until you are good enough, you should come to the realization you have a chink in your armor. Under pressure, that chink manifests itself. When you a see a tour player needing to hole a three footer to win their first tournament, have they truly become good enough to hit a three-foot putt no matter what the conditions? If they have done that, they are going to make it. If they haven't done it, they are probably still not good enough to make it and they have not really practiced under pressure. They have not re-created and simulated those same pressure moments both on and off the golf course for them to succeed.

> *"Through your calmness you can see all the variables with a putt."*

What are the characteristics and attitudes that make a great putter?
I have seen it with the young guys on tour now, as well as with high school, college, and young tour pros. They just putt, putt, putt, with no fear of missing the putt. As you get older and accumulate more memories of missed putts, you might be a little shaken over a putt because you know the odds are against you. That's just been your experience over time.

Other characteristics are being fearless and being calm. Through your calmness you can see all the variables with a putt. It can be argued there are more variables with putting than there are with any other golf shot. In order to digest those variables, you have to be cool, calm, and collected. You have to be able to digest those variables into a mathematical equation in your head to know hard should I hit it, in what direction, and what is the ball going to do? If you are panicky and not calm, you are going to forget about a lot of variables. You have to have an adept touch. There are certain people that are going to be great putters, simply because their touch and feel is keener, more acute than other people. That's just the way we are built as humans—some people run faster than others, some people run longer distances better than others. The same can be said for golfers. Some golfers are great ball strikers though they may not have the touch to be a great putter. Some are great putters and their ball striking is what kills them. It's a rare merge of ball striking and putting that creates an outstanding golfer and we all know who those people are. We look at golfers throughout history and they had that touch and great ball striking abilities. So in order to be a great putter you've got to have the touch, the feel, the dexterity to take in the variables, to be fearless, and to stand over a putt and be very confident.

> *"If you can stand over a putt and you've got all the confidence in the world, odds are you will make the putt."*

The last characteristic is confidence. If you do not have confidence in yourself to do something, who is going to do that something for you? Nobody. You are going to have to find some way of being confident enough to know, "I can hit a four-foot putt in the hole, nine out of 10 times," or, "I can hit a 20-foot putt within six inches, 10 out of 10 times." If you can stand over a putt and you've got all the confidence in the world, odds are you will make the putt. Confidence is not about being egotistical, or greedy, or cocky. True confidence is someone that just takes it all in, they are calm, they don't have a fear of losing, a fear of failure, and they are able to execute time in and time out.

If you had to pick one golfer as a role model for putting, who would it be, why, and what makes them a good role model?
Over the past 10-15 years, Tiger Woods' skills as a putter are undervalued. When the pressure is on, Tiger has shown he is one of the best putters the world has ever known. And there are reasons why.

When you look at roles models for putting, you have to consider a putters consistency. You have to look at guys and gals that have won a lot of major championships, not just one or two. You have to look at the players that are consistently executing on the money list time in and time out.

Another unsung player, believe it or not, is Tom Kite. A lot of people don't realize he was the all-time money winner on tour for a long time until Greg Norman and subsequently Tiger came around. The reason why he enjoyed that position is Tom Kite is an outstanding putter. He wasn't long off the tee, but he is very accurate. He relied on his putting for him to be consistent. There are numerous players out there we can all name that have the characteristics that make them very confident and very calm over whatever putt they may be trying to execute. When you are looking for a role model, those are the two characteristics you have to really look for.

Putts within 10 feet are the most stressful. How should golfers approach this situation, especially to avoid the dreaded 3 putt?
Well first off, let's define why someone 3 putts a green. That's a question we ask all our students at our schools; "Why does a 3 putt happen?" Most people do not answer

this question correctly. They typically say, "Because I missed the second putt." Well, yeah you did; action versus reaction. If your second putt was a reaction, the action to it was you didn't execute your first putt properly. When you really look at it from there, to avoid a 3 putt, you are really going to have to execute your first putt properly, whether it's 10 feet, 100 feet, 2 feet, or anything in between.

A lot of people expect to make a 10 footer. If you look at tour averages of 10-foot putts made by the best players in the world, collectively their percentages are relatively low based on the average golfer's expectations as they watch a tournament on TV. The current average on tour for making a 10-foot putt is around 40%. As an average golfer, you've got to lower your expectations.

Building on the odds that the average golfer will miss a 10-foot putt more times than not, teachers have been teaching you that it is okay to "get it close." So one of the things we teach people at our schools is, if you want to make a 10-foot putt and eliminate 3 putting from that distance, you can't be thinking about "getting it close." You have to commit yourself to making the putt and do what it takes to make the putt. If you run it by a little bit, that's fine; if you are a little bit short, that's fine, but at that particular moment, that's as much as you can do with that first putt. The reaction of, "Hey I missed my second," you have to understand your tendencies of where your second putts are, and practice making those until your fingers bleed.

> *"The current average on tour for making a 10-foot putt is around 40%."*

Along the line of understanding where your first putt will be if you miss the hole, one of the great, great drills for learning to putt from any distance is a drill you can occasionally see Phil Mickelson do before a round. It is called "The Around the World" drill. You will see Phil putting from three feet, four feet, all around the hole. I have been told stories that Ben Hogan used to do this starting with 10 balls at three feet and he would work his way back to 10-feet trying to hit every ball in before moving back to another distance. If he missed a ball, he would have to start that distance all over again. There are stories told to me by much older golfers than I am, that they have actually seen Hogan out on the practice greens at a tournament practicing 6, 8, 10 footers and asking people to shine their car headlights on the green so he could finish making all 10 putts. This is a fantastic drill for the average amateur to practice from inside three-feet because that is where most all their first putts will be when they miss the hole. Plus it recreates the same pressure situation they will face on the course when needing to make their second putt.

The lesson to be learned here is you have to do everything you can to make your first putt, as successfully as you can. Getting a 10-foot putt to drop more often is having the confidence that no matter if it goes in or not, the second putt I will face is an easy one. You can't be thinking about knocking it close, because if you are thinking about that, you are never thinking about making the putt. If you are thinking about making your first putt, it's much easier to conceive not needing a second putt. If you know your tendencies; you are left typically with a two-foot putt, practicing the two footer as much as you practice the 10 footer will not only avoid 3 putting, but also make the 10 footer drop in the hole more often than not.

> *"This is a fantastic drill for the average amateur to practice from inside three-feet because that is where most all their first putts will be..."*

What do you need to do to be a good putter? Are there any tips, techniques, or tricks, that have really helped you, your students, or the pros?

The around the world drill is fantastic. When you talk about distance control, there's also a drill called the "ladder drill," and that's the understanding of how to hit 10, 20, 30 and 40 foot putts. All you do is place tees in the green, measuring each tee you place in the green at 10 foot increments from the hole. Go as far back from the hole as you wish, with each tee you place in the ground at each 10-foot increment representing the rung of your ladder. Using this drill, hit three to four balls from each rung of your ladder, learning what it takes to hit a 10 footer up a hill or how you should hit a 30 footer down a hill, or how you should hit a 20 footer that breaks left to right, or right to left. You'll begin to understand how to control your distances, which is really paramount. As you learn to control those distances, now all of a sudden, when you are going for that bulls-eye, if you miss the putt, your ball will most likely be six-inches away, not 3+ feet away. Along with the around the world drill, if someone practiced these two drills only, their putting consistency would greatly increase.

What a lot of average golfers do not understand is the tour players spend most of their time at a tournament venue during the days leading to the tournament, at the practice green and around the greens on the golf course, predominantly practicing those two drills. The average golfer also does not realize the inordinate amount of time the players spend Monday through Wednesday of a tournament week getting acquainted with the conditions of the greens.

While in Hilton Head, I was fortunate enough to watch the players make a major transition from arguably the fastest set of greens they play all year — The Masters (Bentgrass greens that stimp between 14 and 15), to a different and slower surface of green — Harbor Town Golf Links

(Bermuda greens that stimp between 9 and 11). With each different set of greens comes a different set of variables, such as grass type, grain, slopes, etc. that the players need to acquaint themselves with quickly, or they do not make a living. If you were to go to a practice round of a tour event, men or ladies, you will see the pros taking a lot of time not only on the practice green, but on all 18 greens of the course. This is to become familiar with the greens and the characteristics of the greens, such as where will the pins be placed each day. But, more importantly, they answer the questions of "How do I control my distances from certain spots on the green to those pin positions? How am I going to make sure I am hitting those two, three, four-foot putts consistently?" Answering these questions around the green is what makes them world-class players. The average amateur golfer would be wise to take a page from the tour players' practice book and spend more time understanding the putting conditions they will face each round, by spending at least a minimum amount of time at the practice green before heading to the first tee.

A low score in golf depends on a variety of clubs, skills, and shots. What do you recommend to balance putting in conjunction with these other demands during a round of golf, such as after a good shot, after a bad shot, or being in a rut?
First, what is your rut; what is your weakness? You have to be able to take statistics of your game first to understand what your weaknesses may or may not be. Of the thousands of people that we serve on a yearly basis, very few come prepared to golf school with a statistical trending of the various aspects of their game. So until you know what your weaknesses are, there's not a whole lot of information that any teacher can provide you to help you overcome those weaknesses.

Pertaining to your good and bad shots, statistically going back to numbers, you will hit a drive 14 times, minimally, on any given golf course; not necessarily a driver, but a drive. Knowing this, you have to understand what is your strongest driving club? Is it the driver? Is it a 3-wood? Is it a hybrid? What can I do to put myself in position to make a good second shot?

Arguably, the short game, or the need for short game, occurs when you miss a green. So whether you are on or off the fairway, what are you doing to actually hit a green? In order to reduce your number of putts, the drive into the fairway is certainly important, your ability to hit the green is certainly important. But do you know the statistical trending of where you miss a green? Most people do not. Do you miss it short or long? Do you miss it left or right? When you miss a green, are you in a chipping situation; a pitching situation? Are you hitting out of a bunker? Are you hitting uphill or downhill? When you start tracking these situations within your game, what you are doing in essence is eliminating the words "good" and "bad" from your game, and replacing those words with the phrase, "I now know what to practice within my short game."

When you put a negative connotation on ideals or concepts, your mind really doesn't grasp the negative, only the action. What you have to do is be able to drop the labels of "good" or "bad" and go on with the thought. "Here *is* my shot." "Here *is* my trend." When you do this, you now have the basic framework of developing a plan to improve any aspect of your game, particularly around the green. If you are going to label a good shot "good" and a bad shot "bad," you might as well accept the fact that you will have disproportionate "high" times and "low" times that you will experience while playing golf. When you eliminate good and bad and put it in just a raw, empirical form of, "Here are my trends. Here's what I tend to do in certain situations. Here are my short game situations," you no longer have ruts or weaknesses, you no longer have good or bad shots, you have a tendency that you play to, to create a smarter, strategic plan to play less shots within future rounds.

What are the realistic expectations of putts per hole, putts per round, or other measures golfers need to follow as they develop their skill?
Your ability to putt well is based on skill-set, not expectations. Expectations lead to one thing and one thing only, failure. Expectations do not include a strategic plan of action. Golfers with expectations are just sitting back and, as the word implies, expecting things to happen. So let's talk about how to begin a plan of action.

A plan starts when a golfer faces the fact that par allows for 2 putts per hole. You have 18 holes on a golf course. Most golf courses are par 72. When you look at it in that way, 50% of all shots that par allows are a putt. That is your starting point.

When you are a higher handicapper, can you execute 36 putts in a round? Some people can; most people can't. Most people don't judge their putting success by this mathematical comparison to par. When someone's skill-set develops and the golfer improves, we typically see par averages coming down. When you are putting 36 times in a round, you are typically breaking 90 more often, but not necessarily consistently. In my experience as golf instructor, and I believe statistical analysis will show it as well, someone who is on the verge of breaking 80 is typically putting 31 to 32 times. It's hard to get that number into the 20's, but if they were to do it, the average score reduces in a more meaningful and emotional way. For example, let's say your scoring average is 81 and your average puts per round is 33. If you reduce your average putts per round to

> *"Expectations lead to one thing and one thing only, failure."*

29, in theory, your stroke average has a very good chance of being reduced to 79, a much more powerful and meaningful number in most golfer's minds.

The historical data is there. As you improve statistically within your score, you are going to see your putting averages decline. But when you get to the point of becoming a single-digit handicapper, your ball striking is probably darn good. It's your short game and your putting that will make the most significant differences to improve your scoring average. If your short game can put you closer to the hole so you are not 2 putting, but 1 putting, you'll maintain that average. By the way, 2 putting when you are a single-digit handicapper is the relative equivalent to someone 3 putting when they are a 90's-shooter. You've got to eliminate those 3 putts when you are averaging in the 90's and 80's. You have to eliminate the 2 putts when you miss a green if your stroke average is in the 70's.

> *"It's your short game and your putting that will make the most significant differences to improve your scoring average."*

It really reflects skill level, experience level, and understanding that it's not about expectations. If you have an expectation, you are probably basing it off false information and have no plan to correct your mistakes. In order for you to reach those statistical norms that we see, you have to have a plan of action, you've got to be committed to your practice, and understand the intrinsic value of what putting will do for your overall score.

Looking back, is there anything about putting or golf that you wish you had done differently? What do you know now that you wish you had known sooner?
All the great teachers will tell you they wish they knew

what they know now, when they first started teaching golf because they could have better served the people they taught. I sum that up in a catch phrase: "There's nothing more valuable than experience and there are no shortcuts to experience." So would I do anything over? Absolutely not. I don't have any regrets about anything I have done as a teacher or a player in regards to golf, in particular putting. Having the experience that I have now makes me a more efficient teacher, makes me a more efficient trainer and teacher of teachers. It's not that the people I teach are getting a shortcut; they are just learning from my experiences just as I have learned from my mentors' experiences. It's a maturation process, and for the average golfer, if you try to take a shortcut to that maturation process, you will inevitably fall back to where that shortcut occurred. That's something that we try to have all our students understand. There are no shortcuts; just stick with the plan and you will be fine. No hesitations, no regrets; every day is about learning more and knowledge is power when you know how to use it.

What are your most humbling and memorable putts?
The most memorable are always the ones where you reach a milestone, whether as a club professional passing your PAT, or winning your section championship, qualifying for a tour event, or any other event that has a special place in your heart. Early in my career I played a more competitive game of golf, but golf has always centered on the word "fun" for me.

As far as the humbling and more memorable putts, they come more for me in opportunities of enjoyment and having fun versus competitive. My most memorable ones are typically the ones that my student's make in accomplishing a milestone. Those I can remember like it was yesterday. For me personally, the more memorable putts are the ones on the 18th hole when, after I sank the putt, I am taking my hat off and shaking the hands of the people I have played with simply because I shared that time with them. The knowledge or stories told during that round of golf — those are truly the most memorable. I don't have one in particular that stands out more than any others because they are all truly memorable to me. Collectively, all my putts are very memorable because it allows me to continue the journey of playing golf and learning not only about the game, but about myself.

What would you hope that golfers take away from this interview?
The value of putting — the numerical value of putting, the importance relative to your skill level and how that importance increases in value as you become more skilled. The ratio of that value remains the same no matter what your skill level. In a proportionate way with all skill level of players, it's still all the same based on par normally being 72 strokes. You have 18 holes, so par allows you 2 putts per hole. That is probably the most striking thing that I have learned early on as a golfer that has hit home with me throughout my entire career. You must gain that understanding in order to make a commitment to better putting habits and practicing those habits, to increase your value as a putter. The more knowledge you have of your putting the better off you are going to be as a putter. The better player you become, the more important putting becomes to maintaining that skill level and moving on to the next.

Second, base your putting habits in a simplistic core value of setup positions, something I didn't really talk much about. Everyone sets up differently for a putt. If you look at Palmer and Nicklaus, they are complete opposites as to how they set up. You've got Chi Chi Rodriguez who jabs at it. There is Loren Roberts who has one of the more rhythmic strokes ever. All four are exceptional putters. There's tons and tons and tons of ways of putting. But if you are not set up correctly, if you are not hitting the sweet spot most often (if not all the time), and being able to control your distances, those are really the three most basic skill sets one can learn.

Is there anything else you want to share? Anything you think may help fellow golfers?
There is one thing: Everybody plays golf for one common reason and that's to have fun. In order for you to improve, what you do as a golfer has got to be fun. Whether it's practicing your putting, hitting more fairways, or picking your partners that you play with, are all great examples of fun. You are not going to call up somebody whom you don't enjoy spending time with and go out and play 18 holes of golf. It's a quintessential example of fun. When it comes to improving your game, enjoying the game more holistically, that if you anchor everything in the word "fun" you can't go wrong. If you are anchoring your enjoyment based on, "I have got to work harder at it," or, "I have to think through this in deeper layers," you are going to lose the true value of why you play golf, and that's fun.

> *"...tends to over think things and make things more complicated than they actually are."*

I would say that most every person that comes to our golf school tends to over think things and make things more complicated than they actually are. They tend to read into situations or shots, items or variables, that just don't exist. That's because they are trying to make the game brain surgery or rocket science or something that is beyond any of our capabilities. If you root everything back to the word fun, you improve faster and you enjoy the game more. "Did I have fun practicing my putting today?", "Did I have fun playing with my buddies?", "Did I have fun with the people that engaged me at the golf course?" All are valid questions to ask about your experiences playing golf. When it comes to your improvement, did you have fun improving your golf game?

That's really, in a nutshell, how you are going to get the most out of this. Because if you are not of the same capabilities and skill sets of the people we see every Sunday on TV, vying for millions of dollars, you are not going to have fun doing it. And if you ask every one of those guys, yes it's their job, they will tell you point blank that they truly have fun at what they do. The ones that don't have fun are the ones you don't see on TV—they are maybe the guy that had to take an insurance job or a sales job, or maybe they are the ones teaching at a club they grew up at and wish they could be on TV. At some point along the line, they lost the idea that it should be played for enjoyment, for fun. If you keep that in mind as you go about your improvement process, there's nothing but positives that can happen.

Shim Lagoy
Orinda CC Master PGA Professional

"We spend money on drivers but we should be spending the money on putting."

Shim is one of the 210 original certified Master PGA professionals, has been golfing for over 58 years and now instructs about 300 students per year. Shim is a leader in the 100 holes of golf program to help raise money for the Folds of Honor and Patriot Day promotion.

- Orinda Country Club PGA Professional since 1992
- PGA Master Professional, Member 32 Years
- Recognized as NCPGA Golf Professional of the Year 2003
- Recognized as NCPGA Merchandiser of the Year 1989, 2007
- USGA Senior Open 2002
- 100 Holes of Golf Leading Contributor in State of California, 2009
- Certified TPI Fitness Professional
- Certified V-1 Video Coaching/Instructor

www.orindacc.org

There are millions of new and high handicapped golfers playing every year. How do these golfers need to view the importance of putting in their game?
It's at least, if not more than, half of the game for a lot of people. So the ability to try to become somewhat proficient is a premium if you want to have an enjoyable golf career. One of the things I always tease people about is when they come in and buy that brand new $475, $500, $600 or up to $1,000 driver which they only strike, in a lot of cases, 14 times a round. You should be paying $300 or $400 for that putter that you use anywhere from 25 to 40 times a round, depending on your proficiency. It seems to make more sense to me, to buy the expensive putter and less sense to buy the crazy, long knock driver, or whatever you want to call it. We spend money on drivers but we should be spending the money on putters, if not more so.

The putt can be the most important, most frustrating, and most misunderstood and least practiced shot in golf. What are the key things about the putt that every golfer needs to understand to build a base for accurate, consistent, and enjoyable putting?
One of the things I work on the most is how big is your backstroke and how big is your forward stroke, to effectively keep your putter moving in a decent rhythm, so that you don't flinch on it, you don't flip it, etc. You need to have a way to have a power indicator of how far back and how far forward you go in relationship to your stance; a 14-to-16-inch wide stance between your insteps is preferred. A 12-foot putt is going to be a certain distance backstroke that you can rely on for a level surface. Then the back stroke is a little longer for a 20 footer. But it gives you an indication about how far

> *"We spend money on drivers but we should be spending the money on putters, if not more so."*

back the putter needs to swing with its own free weight to swing back and hit the ball forward the distance you are expecting. The power behind a putt is the most important thing—developing a method that is easy to do under pressure and can consistently be reproduced.

You hear about golfers throwing and breaking putters over missed putts. What are the biggest mistakes you see golfers make that limit their putting ability?
One thing is not being creative when they look at the breaks or what they anticipate the putt might do. I see a lot of people get locked into a very narrow path. They see only one dimension in putting and your good putters will look at a 15 or a 20-foot putt and creatively they will see two or three ways to make it. In their mind's eye they see a straight-forward, flat line putt. They see one with a little bit more broad movement in it, and some will even see, if you think about throwing a frisbee, one that can go way out to the side of the hole and curve back into the cup.

> *"The power behind a putt is the most important thing..."*

Creativity is one of the things that goofs people up and limits their putting ability. It's not just black and white in the narrow channel like an actuary would look at a math problem. The better putters are people with some creative skills, artistic people, sculptors, people who paint, interior designers, people like that. They always seem to be a little bit better at putting, because they seem to have more of a creative mind.

In your experience, what are the road blocks that prevent golfers from becoming good putters?
They take putting for granted. They walk up on the green and whack the ball. It goes straight forward and into the hole. Instead they should be careful, having a precise

approach to it, having the right power, seeing the line, and so on. They take putting for granted until it starts to fail you, and you realize you are a horrible putter.

So now what do you do?
I've changed everything, I have my change in my left front pocket, I've got everything else in my other side pocket, and I've tied my shoes twice. It's like getting rid of the shanks.

Every weekend we see professionals miss simple putts. Why? What is going on that makes them miss these seemingly easy putts?
I believe its concentration. You need to get up and shut that memory bank off for a minute. They have done so many in their lifetime, it's so repetitious. They come up and maybe in a sense don't take that last moment, that last little exhale to make sure that their power is correct with the right amount of power for the backstroke. The right amount of technique, etc. Again, they go up and their concentration fails them. Sometimes it could be attitude; maybe you had a poor performance on the hole before and you are carrying a little baggage. Maybe you're a little irked and now you are trying to make that birdie putt to get you back in the money, back in the driver seat. And then you miss what you think is a relatively easy one, so you go up and sort of matter-of-factly take a pass at it, and there again, attitude sometimes comes along with concentration.

What are the characteristics and attitudes that make a great putter?
Being positive. I have a little piece of paper right next to my telephone I look at every day. As an instructor, I have had about 18 months of the putting woes where it seems like things just aren't going right. I miss some short putts and I am dealing with a number of these things that are in your questions. One of the things I do is I look at this piece of paper every time I answer the phone and it says

very simply, "I am a great putter." It reinforces your confidence. I know I am a good putter, I just happen to be going through a period of time where something in my alignment or something in my technique is not as good as it could be. I try to practice and refine those things, use the different putting tools that are out there and the different elements you could use to help you. But getting myself convinced, again, that I am not a bad putter—I am a good putter.

The attitude for a great putter is they feel like they are a great putter. They feel like they are going to make more than they are going to miss. Our students figure, "Oh man, I haven't made a putt in so long," it's that whole other side of the ledger.

If you had to pick one golfer as a role model for putting, who would it be, why, and what makes them a good role model?
Boy, it would be hard not to pick Brad Paxton. He has consistently putted very well. He and Stan Utley are probably two of the better people that have just consistently been great putters. They have had really reliable strokes. In his recent years, in the five to eight foot range, probably Tiger was as good as anybody. But we can see now that something has changed. I personally think it was the putter, not the puttee. The old putter that he won so many crowns with and picked up so many wins with, was pulled out of his bag and he's been trying to use—as part of his endorsements—the Nike putter and I think that affected how he has done in his putting. I don't have anything against Nike; I just think he took something that was obviously his right-hand man and just pulled it out of his bag.

> *"The attitude for a great putter is they feel like they are a great putter."*

Putts within 10 feet are the most stressful. How should golfers approach this situation especially to avoid the dreaded 3 putt?
Again, being confident that what you have chosen is the right line. If you miss the putt on a chosen line, then I keep telling my students, "Pat yourself on the back because you really hit a good stroke, you just misread the putt." Flip the thing to a positive. Don't say, "God I am a terrible putter! I couldn't make this 10-foot birdie putt." No, you hit a 10-foot birdie putt, you played one ball out and went right over the path you picked—you misread the putt; you didn't have a bad putt. They don't take the positive from it.

They do a good putt, it just didn't go in the hole.
What I do to avoid 3 putts is constantly drill my students to try to make sure the initial putt always gets past the back lip of the hole. Most 3 putts are putts you have not made the distance with—you are going 10 feet, 20 feet, 30 feet, whatever it might be, and if the ball has not had the opportunity to get to or bypass the hole, you have no idea what is remaining. When you leave one, four and a half feet short in the dreaded 3 putt zone, you still have all that trepidation of not knowing what that last four and a half feet does. You have a greater chance of missing it than if you had hit it 18-inches by the hole and you saw what happened as it went buy. You can easily go on the other side of the hole, reverse it, turn it around, and knock an 18 incher back in the hole. I am always talking about, to avoid 3 putting, making sure you get past the back lip of the hole. I just say try to make sure it is beyond the hole because then you have a really good chance of making the come-backer.

What do you need to do to be a good putter? Are there any tips, techniques, or tricks, that have really helped you, your students, or the pros?
What I try to do is be a little bit of a fanatic about measuring

my students, making sure their eyes are vertically set up over their putting line. I get nervous when people's eyes are inside or outside the putter line. I will hang a string down with a pencil on it, or I will take a straight edge or a wooden ruler, and I'll hold it between the bridge of their nose—like where their eye piece would be on some glasses or sun glasses. When they address the ball, I will let it hang straight down and see that it is over their marked line on the putter and over the center of the ball. That way I am pretty sure that line, and eye line, are in a pretty close zone to one another. If your eyes are two inches inside the ball I think it's pretty hard to coordinate putting line and eye line to the same four and a half inch cup. I work hard at making sure their eyes are directly in front of the ball, not necessarily a pet peeve, but it's something I work hard on so my students are comfortable with it.

A low score depends on a variety of clubs, skills, and shots. What do you recommend to balance putting with these other demands during a round of golf, such as after good shots, bad shots, or being in a rut?
I try to recommend to people to practice in some way that's permanent, not perfect. So I always try to recommend that if you are going to do some practice between rounds or are really competing at a high-level, balance your full game and short game practice with at least a half hour twice a week of pure putting practice. Whether you choose to go around the hole in a clock fashion like Mickelson does, and make 25, 30, 40, 50, or 100 three footers. Whether you choose to work on lines and work on your green-reading techniques, or you choose to work on uphill, downhill, side hill—I always try to say that there has to be a balance between the putting, the full game practice and the short game practice. If you don't spend some time on the putting, you could be the best striker in the world and then you can't get it into the hole. I just always try to find a good balance, especially with my younger students, people who I know are going to compete. I have some kids

that compete in junior golf tournaments and do that kind of stuff, so I just make sure they are dedicating some time to that short game and putting portion, along with the long game and the full speed shots.

What are the realistic expectations of putts per hole, putts per round, or other measures golfers need to follow as they develop their skills?
As you work with young people and competitive people that are trying to go to the highest level, their expectation is to hit a lot more greens in regulation. Ideally, I would like to have a high competitor hit 12-15 greens a round. Let's say the three you miss, if you hit 15 greens, you can get it up or down 2/3 of the time. So you have 4 putts there—two single putts and a double—and now you have 15 holes. If I can get them to less than 2 putts per hole, 1.8 or 1.75, now you are talking about the potential for a sub-par round. If I can put one bogie in there, minimize 3 putts, or actually wipe them out totally, I can get three or four 1 putts in those 15 greens they hit. So if I can get all twos, 11 twos would be 22 and four single putts would be 26. Then I have four if I figure two up and down putts where I didn't get it done. I am looking at 30 putts. That's not equating if one of those might have been an eagle putt—if you have a single digit or low handicap or pro-quality player, you may get a green and a five-par in regulation with a single putt for that eagle. Now you are adding one or more two-unders. So I kind of hope they can hold somewhere at 30 and below. And that's tough; that takes a lot of concentration and a lot of hard work. The more greens you miss—unless you are a real accomplished short game player with a high up and down percentage—you are going to have a 2 putt on a lot of those missed greens or bunker shots, that you up and down and won. A sand save. So now you are starting to drill those putts more up to 22, 23, 24 and you are starting to talk about not getting sub-par but getting par or over.

Looking back, is there anything about putting or golf that you wish you had done differently? What do you know now that you wish you had known sooner?
When I started playing, I was very wristy. Sort of a Billy Casper or somebody in the late 1950s or early 1960s. That came in an era when the greens weren't groomed like they are today and they didn't have the technique and equipment that they have now, or the infrastructure of the greens. You had a more au' natural approach. A stimp meter might have been an 8 or an 8.5, so I learned to play with quite a wristy approach. Today as an older player that is something I have to be careful of. I get too wristy, too often. So when I have a bad or a less than adequate putting day, it's usually because I have too much wrist involved and I haven't worked hard on letting the weight of the putter swing, letting it be a more natural stroke. If I had known that sooner, that in the future the greens were all going to be 12 to 14 on a stimp meter, be 6,000 square feet, and have buried elephants in them. If my mechanics had been a little better as a young player in the 1950s and 1960s, I think I would have fared a little better. At this particular time in my life I feel like my putting is not at its peak.

What are your most humbling and memorable putts?
One of my most memorable, happened just a year ago when I was playing at St. Andrews with a bunch of my members. With one of the early par-fives, I almost knocked it on in two. I hit just six or seven-inches from the front putting surface and of course over there you hit a lot of bump and run type putts off the ground. My caddy said, "This is too far to chip; I think you are better off putting." I putted it up where it actually hung on the lip for an eagle. I just went in and tapped in a very short putt. I thought, "That's not too bad. I will take that from this distance because it's not something we are used to." As the typical North American golfer if you are north of the Mason-Dixon Line, the courses are usually so damp and so well aerated that

you rarely hit some type of a bump and run putt shot. You might hit it in the Southwest, Florida, Arizona or southern California, but you don't tend to hit those up in the North. So just getting up there and having something like that turn out pretty well in one of those spots you are not used to doing it in, it was great.

When I think about the most humbling, I think about being in putting situations where there is a large grade in front of you and maybe you have tried to put up a shelf or something and it's rolled back to you again and you have to do it over. Everybody has had one or two of those in their life. You thought you hit the right putt and watched it roll right back and you've got to do it all over again.

What do you hope golfers take away from this interview?
Just to develop some confidence, don't be so hard on themselves. "I am worthy." It's not, "I'm not worthy to be a good putter." But, "I am worthy to be a good putter. I work hard at it." And if they could just take the time to put in a little putting practice; it's not easy to practice because it's kind of an uncomfortable position to stand in for a period of time. It's not a lot of fun to repetitively hit putts, so I try and develop some games with my students. If you want them to take something away from this, develop a couple of games that you play. Don't just stand there and hit eight or nine five-footers up a hill. Move the ball around—putt a 10 footer, putt a four footer, putt an 11 footer, putt a five footer, and put some parameters on it. Take a score card with you. Play nine holes on your club's practice green and try for 18 putts or less. Pick out a different hole each time and go through your procedure: line it up, pick your line, walk in just as though you were playing with your buddies for this week's coke, beer round or this week's $5 Nassau. Go through the whole

> *"...take the time to put in a little putting practice..."*

process like you are on the course just playing around; make that nine holes of practice putting something that is going to be good for you. Not just, "Well, I am going to practice out here for a half hour or so and just check my brain out for a while and whack a few balls on the putting green." Make it productive.

Is there anything I didn't ask that you feel I should be asking?
No, you have a lot of great points here. I agreed to talk to you because I saw some things that I thought people don't usually ask. You covered a lot of areas that will help people. Hopefully it makes them enjoy putting a little more, enjoy what they are doing, and play more golf.

Becky Dengler
LPGA Master Golf Teaching Professional

"If you can't putt and make three footers, you are going to struggle with everything else."

Throughout her career, Rebecca Dengler has been recognized by numerous golfing organizations, publications, and her colleagues for her positive, innovative teaching style. Most recently, she was named in the Golf Digest 50 Best Women Teachers in America (19th). The LPGA named her one of the country's 50 Top Teachers for 2008-09. There were more than 1,200 teaching professionals around the country voted on to compile this list. In 2007-2008 Becky was named the #1 teacher in the state of Delaware by Golf Digest Magazine. She has also been named a top teacher by Golf for Women and Golf Magazine. In 2010 she was also included in the US Kids Top 50 Teachers list for her third time.

Becky's philosophy of golf teaching has been greatly influenced by some of the elite teachers in the game. Becky traveled to Sweden to spend time with golf instructors who influenced Annika Sorenstam and other Swedish players. She has studied the methods of great teachers like Fred

Shoemaker, author of *Extraordinary Golf*. Most recently, Becky has been working with Ed Feeney, an author and behavioral change expert, to further improve her skills and effectiveness as an instructor.

- PGA/LPGA Teaching Professional
- Ed Oliver Golf Club
- PGA Class A Member Since 1991
- LPGA Class Member Since 1993
- Body Balance for Performance certified
- PGA Golf Psychology Certified
- 2008 Philadelphia Magazine Top 25 Teachers in the Area
- 2010 US Kids Top 50 Teacher for the Third Time
- Golf Digest 50 Best Women Teachers in America 2010-11 (19th)
- Golf for Women Top 50 Teacher
- Golf Magazine Top Teacher by Region
- Contributor to Philaldelphia Golfer Magazine and Various Other Publications

www.rebeccadengler.com

There are millions of new and high handicapped golfers playing every year. How do these golfers need to view the importance of putting in their game?
Mark Brody did a lot of research about the effects of the short game and putts to scoring, and the PGA has now converted their putting stats system because of Mark Brody's research. But to the amateur golfer, you are easily looking at putting at least 40% of all your shots. As Mark Brody would say, "Yeah, but a pro player is going to make every three footer." But what he is missing is that amateurs can get close to missing three-footers 50% of the time, if they putted them out. It's a huge part. If an amateur cannot make a three-foot putt, they probably do not have a great relationship to club face, their hands, the

ball, the hole—just on a straight, flat putt. If they don't have that relationship at three feet with a putter in their hand, they are going to struggle with irons, full swings, drivers—everything.

I have heard that as well—the putt isn't a stand-alone thing. It's similar to the relationship you have with every other club you have.
Yes, it happens in such a small space and slower time span. If the regular amateur doesn't have control over that type of a shot, they are really going to struggle with everything else.

The reason for the question is, I don't think most people, when they start out, understand that relationship.
In my experiences, especially with a new golfer, they are expecting to come to their first lesson and be taken to the driving range. They probably think they are going to learn to take a full swing with their driver on their first swing. Once I talk to them about the game and lay it out for them I say, "You are welcome to start putting a three-foot putt," and they look at me most of the time with such relief in their eyes. They were scared to death of swinging and missing, and then being embarrassed, not being successful. It's an easier pill to swallow to take them to the putting green and start them at three feet, and they love it. They can be successful.

The putt can be the most important, most frustrating, most misunderstood and least practiced shot in golf. What are the key things about the putt that every golfer needs to fully understand to build a base for accurate, consistent, and enjoyable putting?
Well, in terms of cognitive understanding, on a flat putt, the main influence on the ball is the putter face in terms of direction. Secondly—the timing of the stroke and the length of stroke. Overall, it's the ability to maintain

a stroke that is very consistent in terms of timing and tempo—along with the direction of the putter face.

You hear about golfers throwing and breaking putters over missed putts. What are the biggest mistakes you see golfers make that limit their putting ability?
Their ability to attend to what needs to be attended to in putting. In other words, if they are set up over the ball, they have already planned where they are going to putt it—which a lot of people don't do—from behind the ball. They have the ability to set up and make a proper read—that would be AimPoint information. And then they are able to, skill-wise, start the ball on the intended line and their brain has the information of the distance from the ball to the hole. All of that has to be taken in at the right time and place, to execute a putt well. For a good putter, all those things are in place—the green, the setup, the ability to set the ball on the intended line, and the ability to perceive the distance the ball needs to travel. That gets communicated to your body and your stroke.

In your experience, what are the road blocks in preventing golfers from becoming good putters?
Their internally focused attention. In other words, if they are focused on the ball, if they are focused on their stroke, if they are focused on the mechanics—anything other than what needs to be attended to, they are not going to be able to take in that information and execute well. Basically, a lot of amateur golfers who have trouble with distance generally are looking at the ball too long. They haven't viewed the space between the ball and the hole within less than five seconds of making the stroke. The brain literally just doesn't have that space. It's just pure physiology—except when you come down to blind people. But blind people do a have a relationship, probably a sharper one, to the target.

I have heard that blind golfers have a much, much, much, higher perception of what is between the ball and the hole, than people that use their eyes.
Correct. Debbie Cruz did a bunch of testing with people putting. She said the best putter she ever worked with was a blind woman. This woman could just drain putts anywhere. To this day she still calls her the best putter she has ever seen — just an amateur woman who was a blind putter. She also tracked exactly what parts of her brain were active. The woman said she could see the putt — so when she could 'see' the hole, the part of her brain that was activated was the part that would indicate vision, even though she was blind.

Every weekend we see professionals miss simple putts. Why? What is going on that makes them miss these seemingly easy putts?
Well, one explanation is that a lot of times the professionals can be so pumped up they literally just create too much velocity. The ball hits the back of the hole and doesn't fall in, because of their adrenaline.

The others, going back to AimPoint information, a lot of these guys and girls don't know that they couldn't start the putt on the intended line. They think they are great putters and there are still one or two basic things that are still missing in their stroke that they don't realize. One being the ability to start a foot and half on your intended line, and the weight of the putter versus the speed of the greens.

They just don't have all the variables figured out.
Correct. They kind of work around them, but don't know it.

What are the characteristics and attitudes that make a great putter?
A positive perception that they are going to make the putt.

Any thought of it not going in is just not good. Generally, a positive attitude and a pace in terms of not being rushed. A lot of women, if they feel rushed or if someone is behind them, have an attitude of, "I've just got to get out of the way." They are not going to putt well.

In tournaments you can watch somebody putt, putt, putt, and they will be at a certain pace. Then they will hit a hole and have either a faster or slower cadence than their normal process, and they will miss it by a ball-width or so. You can tell they have changed something, because they are not moving at the same speed and they are not doing the same process that they have done before.

Debbie has done a lot of work in terms of routine and set-up. There's a company called Eyeline Golf and they have a little metronome you attach to your shirt. They recommend using it when you are behind the ball to help set your pace. You might have 1/64th beat, which is a decent beat for a putting stroke. So you would walk up to the ball at that same pace, and it allows you to set up with more care and precision. This is the line between the amateurs and the pros. The time and the care that I would take to set up my putter to the ball, you just don't find that with amateurs.

If you had to pick one golfer as a role model for putting, who would it be and what would make them a good role model?

I probably would have to go with someone a little older, like an Anika Sorenstam. I am familiar with their philosophy. Back then the Swedish team decided they were great putters and they were going to 1 putt everything. That was her philosophy. I think that type of mentality creates success in the stroke. A putting stroke just isn't too complicated to me. It's been described as a simple motor skill, like tying your shoe laces. When you have somebody like an Anika, that approached putting with a whole different mentality, that she is going to make every putt, makes a better golfer.

Putts within 10 feet are the most stressful. How should golfers approach this situation especially to avoid the dreaded 3 putt?
Any player that would like to perform well would need to spend some time at three-foot putts and be able to make them 90% of the time. If not, you've got stroke issues, you have mental issues; you probably have lots of issues. But just becoming successful 90% of the time at three footers, will set the stage. Now, if you want your putting stats to get better and better, you can then stretch that out to four or five feet. But you need to keep a realistic mentality of how many putts a really good putter is going to make at 4, 5, 6, 7, 8, 9, 10 feet. Amateurs think they should make most of their 10 footers. So, to have some basis of skill at three feet, and then build on that would very simply be aim, square putter face at impact, the ability to perceive distance, and pace.

What do you need to do to be a good putter? Are there any tips, techniques, or tricks, that have really helped you, your students, or the pros?
Mechanically, it's a very simple stroke with movement indicated in the shoulders, and shoulders only. This is not easy for a lot of people. A lot of times, people can't rotate at their shoulders without moving their wrist or their body. So the ability to just rotate the arms at the shoulder joint—nothing else moves—that's the basic mechanics. Then to have a stroke that slightly accelerates, and then on top of that have a plan that is accurate, to be successful at six inches past. In AimPoint, it's six inches past and it's also based on the read of the low point, where gravity would go, and finding your angle to that. It can get a little complicated, but if you know some basic AimPoint principles it makes a lot of sense. It's just pure physics.

A low score in golf depends on a variety of clubs, skills, and shots. What do you recommend to balance putting in conjunction with these other demands during a round of golf, such as after good shots, after bad shots, or being in a rut?

I would probably just default back to that routine that we talked about—keeping the same pace in your routine, having a very clear plan. Even if you just screwed up the last shot—and it's going to happen—if you can get right back to your good routine at your proper pace, then the wheel doesn't fall off. That's the thing that keeps everything going.

Golfers may have a couple of bad holes and they will say "I will just birdie these next two," and they will get over-aggressive and get into trouble.

In any of those behaviors, we would see a change in their pace; we would see a lack of planning or attention to other things that don't really matter. So they just get distracted. They didn't carefully set up their putter. They would probably be rushing.

What are the realistic expectations of putts per hole, putts per round, or other measures that golfers need to follow as they develop their skills?

For a new player, I would like them to make 50% of their three footers and then we get them somewhat competent in 2 putting beyond three feet. Then a basic chip for a good player is going to average about three feet, so I will give an amateur nine feet, but then they are going to 2 putt. Therefore, they are going to get a three from just off the green, which is going to meet the standards of most average players. Then we just build the swing from there. Moving tees forward has helped a lot, especially for women since it has them playing at a more appropriate length. If they are playing 4,500-yards and they can hit a 150-yard tee shot, and they can do three from off the green, they are either going to be shooting par, or bogie. And I can get ANY woman hitting a ball 100-150 yards—that's not a problem.

Is there anything about putting or golf that you wish you had done differently? What do you know now that you wish you had known sooner?
I wish I knew about AimPoint much sooner. If I had learned that as one of my first cornerstones, that would have made everything much easier. It really does come down to science and people aren't learning where to aim and why to aim and their brain really doesn't know what speed to putt. So, I wish I had had that green-reading information sooner. I still think the putters are a big issue and I like the Dave Edell putting system. People don't realize how much their putter is affecting them. I do putter fitting to the best of my ability. I have different putters and people try them; I see how they aim, we check the weight in terms of how they can throw the pace, but I am at a public golf course with slower greens. So putter fitting is a big variable that you have to deal with along with the stroke.

What are your most humbling or memorable putts?
One comes to mind recently. I was in a Pro-am that my team ended up winning. On the 18th hole, it was a five-some, my four amateurs are putting and they are good putters and nobody made it in—probably a 20 footer. So I knew exactly where it had to break, I had seen 4 putts in front of me, and that's the case where you just set it up and get it going on the right line at the right speed. It went in and it should have. It's nice to see because you have all the information and you have to create that whole scenario on your own. I kind of imagine a ball rolling on the green to the hole and where would it go, things like that. You have to create all that.

> *"Moving tees forward has helped a lot, especially for women..."*

But our team won the Pro-am and that was good. I am pretty sure it came down to that putt.

What do you hope that golfers take away from this interview?
That they can now put their attention to things that really matter. Take time and care to set up, know where to putt and then have the ability to putt it there with a simple, mechanical stroke. I don't think that is a putting lesson most people get. I am not saying people teach wrong things, I just think a lot of amateurs aren't getting taught putting. I don't know if teachers feel like they don't know how to teach putting. I remember I was at one golf school on the putting green and it was a busy place. They kept coming to me and I had a group and they said, "Tell us when you need the range." "Okay." A while goes by, I am on the putting green, putting, chipping, pitching and they kept wondering. At one point a bunch of the players were just standing there watching me and I know they were thinking, "What is she doing? All morning on the putting green?" So, I would hope this would give golf pros some information on what to teach so that they address it more regularly.

> *"...a lot of amateurs aren't getting taught putting."*

Is there anything else you would like to share? Anything you think may help?
There's a company that most people are not aware of called Edell Putters. Dave Edell makes custom made putters. They use lasers to figure out all these things and it's just some really, really neat stuff about you and your putter.

He is just incredible. He has gone through so many fittings with people and it's very fascinating. My next putter will be an Edell Putter, but they are very expensive. They go anywhere from $300 to $500 and there are only a certain number of fitting kits around the country. It's hard to get into that situation, but to me that is the ultimate. Now, it may not be perfect for everyone, but still, if you want to eliminate the factor of the putter to the best of your ability that would be what I would go with.

Carol Preisinger
Golf Magazine Top 100 Teacher in America, 2005-Present

"Do you love your putter?"

Carol's talent in playing the game was nurtured by her father, George, now a retired life member of the PGA. So Carol virtually grew up in a golf shop. Carol received her Class A status in 1992, and achieved Master status in 2010. Carol is currently the director of golf instruction at the Kiawah Island Club. She is active in corporate golf and motivational outings, LPGA programs, seminars and workshops. She is currently serving as president of the LPGA Southeast Section for teaching and club professionals, elected in 2010, and sits on the LPGA Executive Committee. Carol has contributed to many golf publications, including GOLF Magazine, Golf Digest, served on the instruction panel for Golf For Women Magazine, and has appeared on various occasions on The Golf Channel's "Golf Academy Live" with Mike Ritz and on "Your Game Night" with Kelly Tilghman. Carol is a member of the Nike Golf Swoosh Elite staff and serves on Nike Golf's Women's Advisory Board.

- GOLF Magazine Top 100 Teacher in America, 2005—Present
- Golf Digest Top 50 Best Women Teachers, 2010
- Golf Digest Best in State SC, 2007, Voted #1 2009
- LPGA Top 50 Teacher, 2008
- Golf for Women Top 50 Teachers, 2000-2007
- Golf Digest Best in State Georgia, 2000, 2003
- LPGA National Teacher of the Year, 1998
- LPGA Southeast Section Teacher of the Year, 1998

www.carolpreisinger.com

There are millions of new and high handicapped golfers playing every year. How do these golfers need to view the importance of putting in their game?
New and high handicapped golfers have to understand that the putting green is the last place you want to spend a lot of time on when you're playing. You need to get a good feeling of what it is to make a good putting stroke, and control speed. Today's greens are very undulated and faster than they were 15-20 years ago. So they need to understand that once they learn how to play the game, the full swing is only 1/5 of what they do out there. They also have to learn the basics of the chip, the pitch, the bunker shot, but putting is going to be at least 50% of their score right away. If they can manage themselves on the putting green, they may not know it yet, but that's going to help them chip better, pitch better, and hit the ball better.

> *"...the putting green is the last place you want to spend a lot of time on..."*

The putt can be the most important, most frustrating, most misunderstood and least practiced shot in golf. What are the key things about the putt that every golfer

needs to fully understand to build a base for accurate, consistent, and enjoyable putting?

Before they start to establish a putting stroke, they have to make sure they get properly fitted for a putter. Technology in golf equipment has sky rocketed and most golfers are spending a lot of time and money getting fitted for a driver that they only use 14 times per round. They need to realize they are going to be using their putter 30-40 times a round, so they better get a putter that fits them properly. Only then are they going to be able to find their true putting stroke. They must get the right length because standard length putters at 35 or 36 inches are too long by an inch or two. The problem is, when you cut that putter down, every half inch you take off the length will change the weight by 12 grams, therefore it changes the head weight of the putter and you need to be able to feel the true weight of that putter head. The putter has to be balanced.

The grip size is very important because a lot of people need to calm down their wrists in a putting stroke. That's why you see the popularity of those thicker, fatter grips. Then they need to make a choice of a blade or mallet style head which is going to suit their pace, vision, and feel of the stroke best. Fitting also depends on whether this golfer is visually, auditory or kinetically dominant. Visual learners are going to learn to just say, "I see myself here; there's the hole." They can judge distance very well. Auditory learners have to create that tick-tock rhythm of their stroke. For the kinetic (feel) players, it's almost like a black art because they are just smooth and relaxed and they just feel it. They are cursed because sometimes they are not going to have the feeling that day and they are going to be stuck in a rut with putting. There's so much feel involved and so many preferences involved, it has to be student centered for each golfer to find the key things about their putt.

In my observations, people will buy a $19 putter that's on sale at a discount store, or get a hand-me-down putter,

and what has emerged is the fitted putter. Are you saying that people ought to get a fitted putter right from the start?
Yes, because if the putter does not fit the golfer, the golfer will start to make compensations in their setup and putting stroke based on that putter they are using. If the putter is too long or too short, if the head weight is too heavy or too light, the grip too skinny or too fat, if the lie angle is too flat or too upright, they will make compensation in their stroke and create an inefficient stroke.

If the putter is too long, most people will set up taller and their eyes will be inside the line of the putt. Research shows that people tend to miss to the right when their eyes are set up inside the line. Sometimes the putter is too short—which we rarely see. A golfer may bend too far forward and their eyes will be outside the line, and research shows that they will miss left. But the length, the lie angle—those things need to be fitted properly so the player's eyes are as close as they can be over the line, hands under shoulders, comfortable balance and lower body setup that is stable so that they can make a smooth and relaxed putting stroke

> *"Do you love your putter?"*

You have to sit a while and just watch people and how they approach, how they set up and how they do their stroke. I think that backs up your analysis of getting the putter fitted first before you get started.
I truly believe that, because it is the club you are going to use the most during every round you play. You have to ask yourself: Do you love your putter? My students will look at me inquisitively and I will repeat that question. Would you cry if you couldn't find your putter in your golf bag? Every now and then I have someone say, "Oh my God, yes! If I lost this putter I would just die!" Most people say, "I don't know."

You have to love your putter. You have to have confidence in your putter. When you were just talking about seeing different types of people on the green, some people are overloaded with mechanics. They are not instinctively reacting to the green, the stroke, the feel and the distance, and the last thing you want to be thinking is, "Is this the right putter for me? Am I going to make a good stroke?" You have to be committed; you've got to trust, and you've got to love your putter.

You hear about golfers throwing or breaking putters over missed putts. What are the biggest mistakes you see golfers make that limit their putting ability?
Preparation. Golfers must learn how to be quick in preparing for the putts. The more you prepare and have a sense for the speed, where you are going to aim, and how to read greens, the more confident you are going to be. If you happen to miss the putt, you won't be so mad at yourself. I think frustration comes from not being prepared and expecting to make a putt without preparing or practicing. I think people have unrealistic goals for themselves and they have to prepare and have a plan to improve. Putting can be very challenging today because the greens are sloped and fast, and you have to be ready. You also have to learn how to control your emotions.

> *"Frustration comes from not being prepared and expecting to make a putt without preparing or practicing."*

In your experience, what are the road blocks that prevent golfers from becoming good putters?
Misconceptions and overload of mechanics. I had a lady yesterday that thought she had to keep the putter so low on the follow-through, and her shoulders weren't moving at all. Again, I am a very student-centered teacher,

so I never know what to expect with each person. Speed has become the number one issue and certain teachers that just work on pace are very popular now. If golfers can get the speed down, there are still a lot of them that can't aim properly. They have an aim bias. Since I have become certified at Level I with AimPoint Technologies' green reading program that Mark Sweeney developed, I've found that there are so many people that don't really know how to read a green. They need to treat putting as a whole, complete area of the game and try to master it.

> *"Speed has become the number one issue..."*

I'd like to add, regarding the road blocks, that people develop poor mechanics because they are consciously thinking of making the putt versus making a stroke. That is the biggest road block. The putting motion rolls the ball, not hits it. We have heard so many good words as to how it feels when a good stroke is made, and it's different for everybody, but I think that's the one main road block I see: they are hitting a putt versus making a stroke.

Every weekend we see professionals miss simple putts. Why? What is going on that makes them miss these seemingly easy putts?
For professionals, there are a couple things: Number one, we used to say, "If you have a 2-3 footer, take all the break out and just ram it in the back of the cup." Well, you can't do that anymore because the faster that ball is rolling at the hole, the smaller the hole becomes. You will see a lot of those short putts lip out, and that's because of too much speed.

The other thing is they may not take enough time and are not committed. They don't treat that two footer like a 20-footer. I remember watching Cristie Kerr when she won the open at Pine Needles. At 18 she had a two footer to win. She took her time, she marked that ball, she went back, she lined it up, she re-placed her ball, set up, went through her routine—consistent, consistent, consistent. She stayed in the moment, and made that putt.

What are the characteristics and attitudes that make a great putter?
When you talk about attitudes, how many times have we seen Tiger Woods make putts when he had to with sheer willpower? Regarded as one of the greatest putters in the game, he had a stretch there for four or five years on tour where he was ranked #1 in putts made. He just had so much willpower to basically will that ball into the hole. It goes back to confidence and trust and commitment, but you also have to be able to read greens and get the speed down. The main characteristic is confidence, that trust factor, being in the moment and basically willing that ball to go into the hole.

> *"...people develop poor mechanics because they are consciously thinking of making the putt versus making a stroke. That is the biggest road block."*

If you had to pick one golfer as a role model for putting, who would it be, why, and what makes them a great role model?
Ben Crenshaw, the focus that he had, and he controlled his emotions. Ben would get to a putt inside of 10 feet and you knew he was going to make it. Also Jack Nicklaus, similar to Tiger with the willpower and determination to make the putt. I like players that are relatively quick in their process because the less you think about it, the more successful you are. Amateur players who over-think and take too much time to line a putt up, get in their own way.

Putts within 10 feet are often the most stressful. How should golfers approach this situation, especially to avoid the dreaded 3 putt?
Practice! When you are 10 feet out, or closer, your brain will automatically be able to help you judge the speed. You have got to learn to aim properly and you have to read the putt properly. Speed is going to be relatively easy inside of 10 feet. To approach the situation when you are playing, focus on getting that ball started out on the correct line within a foot of the stroke, where the stroke begins. Practice all around the hole, uphill and downhill. Don't practice flat, straight putts because you are hardly ever going to have a flat, straight putt on the golf course. Surround a hole with balls in a clock pattern and putt from 2, 4, 6, 8 and 10 feet out. Get used to the side hill, uphill, and downhill breakers. On the golf course they have to really find the right line and aim properly inside 10 feet.

> *"Don't practice flat, straight putts..."*

What do you need to do to be a good putter? Are there any tips, techniques, or tricks, that have really helped you, your students, or the pros?
You have to have a putter that is fitted and a putter that you love. Now, you've got to be able to create a repetitive stroke. However you set up, whichever grip you use, there are many different techniques and you need to find the one that is best suited to your game, but I can't talk about speed enough. There's a fun drill to do to work on speed control, called the cluster drill. Set three balls up in a row and set up. Do not look at a hole, do not putt to a hole, do not putt to a certain distance consciously in your mind. Just make three repetitive strokes at the same pace, the same length, the same tempo, through each of the three balls. After you have putted the third ball, now look and see if the balls are clustered together. Most amateurs

will begin with the balls 2-feet apart. If you can get them within six inches of each other, that is great speed control.

I also like a little drill called the "Tornado Drill" where you set seven balls around the hole in a spiral. The first ball one foot away, the second ball two feet away, another three feet away, etc., until you create the spiral around the hole. You will practice different lengths of putts, different reads of putts, and different speed of putts. I remember having a discussion with Morris Pickens down at Sea Island. We were talking about 25-30 handicappers having these 40 and 50 foot putts from one section of green to another, with offsetting breaks. He said, "Why would you tell them to try to get it into a three-foot circle when they can make the putt?" I said, "Well, realistically, for that level of golfer, they are most likely not going to make that putt." And he said, "Wouldn't you want them to think they could?" It made me rethink how I teach those long putts. Now, learning what I know from AimPoint, it is so much simpler to read long putts and get the speed right. Now I believe every golfer should get over every putt, and think that they should make it.

> *"...every golfer should get over every putt, and think that they should make it."*

A low score in golf depends on a variety of clubs, skills, and shots. What do you recommend to balance putting in conjunction with these other demands during a round of golf, after good shots, after bad shots, or being in a rut?

To balance putting in conjunction with other skills, the tempo and rhythm of the putting stroke works with your chips and pitches. If you can find that pace, all you are doing is changing the length of the stroke, length of the chip shot, or length of the pitch shot, depending on the distance you want to carry. Mentally and emotionally people need to learn that after a good shot or a bad shot they need to stay in the moment. Whether it is a putt, a chip, a pitch; they have to stay in that moment, concentrate on that moment, and then just execute it. They can't over think it. They shouldn't worry about the bad shot they just hit, and they have to control themselves when they hit a great shot, because adrenaline is going to be pumping. They have to manage their mental and emotional game—and fitness too. People need to stay balanced in their life and balanced in their body. That's a huge issue right now as our core golfer group gets older—the mobility issues and physical limitations are increasing. We as teachers are trying to allow them to play better golf with compatible compensations. With putting, the long putter and belly putter are very popular, because the motion is more pendulum-like and people don't have to lean over as far, it is easier on the back.

Golfers can be doing terrible and then will pull up the score card and look at the next two holes and say, "Well, if I birdie the next two holes I will be back where I want to be." Yet they haven't gotten a birdie all day.
It's an unrealistic expectation when they jump into the future. They need to learn to stay in the moment. Golf has so many external variables we cannot control and internal variables that we need to get better at managing. Every now and then, the stars are all in alignment and we go out and we have one of those days when we are not worried about anything. We are not in a hurry; we are relaxed, we are playing with friends, and boom! We have a great round.

When the heart rate goes up, the body releases cortisol, a stress hormone. When you get angry and mad, cortisol goes into your blood stream and tightens your muscles. I don't know if it's a control issue, but we live in a society where everybody wants to control things and you cannot control your golf swing. You can prepare for it, you can control your choices, you can control where you want to aim, you can control your practice time, but once you get over that ball and you're ready to pull that trigger, you have to let go of the control.

What are the realistic expectations of putts per hole, putts per round, or other measures golfers need to follow as they develop their skills?
I would say each golfer needs to establish a base; if they haven't already charted putts per green they need to start doing that. They need to find out how many putts they are having per round and have that as a base and then establish a goal. Like in the next three months, I want to improve my putting stroke average by two strokes or three strokes, and be very, very realistic. 2 putts per hole is realistic if you practice.

It's hard to throw out numbers for everybody to quantify themselves because everybody is a little different. But I think not only keeping track of putts per hole, but how many times do you miss the green? How close are your chip shots? Chart the length of your putts and how many putts you make within 10 feet, 20 feet, and outside of 30 feet. Most people don't ever practice going from one section of the green to the other. Most of your 3 putts are going to occur from one section of the green to another. You may be coming from an area where downhill is to your right, putting to another section of the green where downhill is to the left. You've got to learn to read those like two separate putts. That's part of the AimPoint process. This would eliminate 3 putts if people can learn how to prepare for long putts as if you are reading two separate putts.

> *"2 putts per hole is realistic if you practice."*

Looking back, is there anything about putting or golfing that you wish you had done differently? What do you know now that you wish you had known sooner?
As a player in college, I wish I had had the right putter for me. I am now on Nike's Swoosh Elite staff and I love my Method putter, but in 1981 I found a Ping-61 offset and I played with that putter for about 22 years. That putter was an inch and half longer than it should have been for me, but I learned to love that putter. I do wish I had gotten fitted properly and I do wish I had learned how to read greens better. If the AimPoint process existed 30 years ago, I probably would have been on tour.

What are your most humbling and most memorable putts?
We have a Solheim Cup format called the Cross-River Cup, where Kiawah Island competes against Briars Creek. I play the teaching professional at Briar's, Eve Vanderweele, who used to play the Futures Tour five years ago. I had a putt on the 18th green to win the first match. It was a three and a half footer, side hill, three-inches break, greens rolling at 11. I was over that putt and I knew I had this putt to win the point, and my heart was pounding out of my throat. I made the putt because I was so focused.

I can remember as a kid on the practice green at the old Marietta Country Club, just seeing the path of the putt. I am a non-linear putter; I see the curve, and I had such visual awareness of seeing the curve of the putt. At the time I had no idea what was happening, I had no idea how great that was; I just saw it and I putted. I will never forget that, and I still see it today.

What do you hope golfers take away from this interview?
I hope one day we can look out on a practice facility and see 8 or 10 golfers on the putting green and two on the range, and that they realize that putting is a true art. It's a combination of judging speed, being able to find the line,

see the line, aim properly, get comfortable. It is an art and you've got to develop your own artistic flair with putting. It takes time. You can see something quickly, you can hear something quickly, but in order to get the feel of something you must do it over and over again. It is trial and error learning. I wish that people would spend more time on their putting and get fitted for a putter.

Is there anything else that you would like to share? Anything you think I have left out that would help your fellow golfers?
One thing came to mind. When people are in the zone, that's when they are having fun. Some people just don't realize it. Everybody has their own personality and when people are playing their best golf, they're in the zone. Sometimes you see people laughing and having fun, sometimes people are focused. When a tour player completes a round, they have been in the zone. They played great and made a lot of putts, and if interviewed, they'll say, "You know, I really had fun out there today."

> *"I hope one day we can...see 8 or 10 golfers on the putting green and two on the range..."*

Dan Schwabe
Northern California
PGA Teacher of the Year

"I would like people to learn to putt more like a six-year-old."

Dan is a PGA Class A golf professional who has taught over 35,000 (and counting) golf lessons, and currently teaches about 2,500 to 3,000 students in group and individual sessions each year. In addition, Dan has played tournament golf for over 25 years. He has been teaching golf at the Presidio Golf Course for over 12 years, and during that time has become one of the busiest instructors in the country and most recognized instructors in northern California.

Dan was awarded Northern California PGA Teacher of the Year in 2009.

www.danschwabe.com

There are millions of new and high-handicapped golfers playing every year. How do these golfers need to view the importance of putting in their game?

The average person will come in and say that they are not that bad at putting, because relative to their driving, where they hit it really far offline, their putting only misses by a few feet side to side. So they don't think they are very bad putters. They really need to recognize how many strokes putting is relative to their total strokes, what percentage it is, and then realize how little they practice their putting. Take that, and compare it to how much they try to work on their swing, whatever that might be, they don't practice proportionally in the correct amount to their putting as it affects their golf score.

The putt can be the most frustrating, most misunderstood, and least practiced shot in golf. What are the key things about the putt that every golfer needs to fully understand to build a base for accurate, consistent, and enjoyable putting?

The simplest idea is to learn how to control your speed and find the middle of the putter face. Find a consistent sweet spot on the putter and be able to control how far you hit your putts. That is the number one key to reducing 3 putts — reading greens and angling the putter face are all totally related, but if you can't control your speed you are going to leave yourself with short putts, long putts, and sloped putts. You are not getting the ball into the right speeds of the break needed to get it to finish in the right direction and right distance. So speed and hitting the center of the face is just absolutely critical.

> *"The average person will come in and say that they are not that bad at putting..."*

You hear about golfers throwing and breaking putters over missed putts. What are the biggest mistakes you see golfers make that limit their putting ability?

They are too tight, too tense, and they move around too much. They don't relax their minds, get a more comfortable, focused rhythm, have a good routine, and relax.

In your experience, what are the road blocks that prevent golfers from becoming good putters?
Too many thoughts. After a while, making a 10-foot shot in basketball, after you have done it enough, you are not thinking about the 20 things that are moving in your body. A lot of times the road blocks are that people are thinking about controlling it a lot more than working on rhythm, focus, relaxation, and being able to control their speed. Whether people believe or not in left sided or right sided brain; if they are in the left side of their brain and really consciously controlling everything, they need to find a way to get a routine and a rhythm that allows them to get a little more unconscious. They need to move that putter with a lot more freedom and trust than with them consciously controlling every movement.

> "...move that putter with a lot more freedom and trust..."

Every weekend we see professionals miss simple putts. Why? What is going on that makes them miss these seemingly easy putts?
Well, tension, nerves, misalignment to a putter face—if something has slightly gotten off with their setup or mechanics and so forth. But more importantly when even the best of putters get offline for a while, their focus is off and they miss and their mind is not as free and clear as it needs to be. They are probably focusing their attention on results and outcomes more than just the simple relaxation and rhythm of finding the center of that face. I know I come back to that more and more, but it's the truth. You can have a technically fantastic putting stroke and if you are distracted, anxious, worried, or afraid of the outcome

or results, you can absolutely neuro-muscularly flinch because you are afraid to miss.

So the whole idea is if you are over a putter, and you are thinking about how you have missed putts and you don't want to miss, it's like thinking about wanting to avoid a car wreck in your car. Eventually you are going to tense up and you are going to be very uncomfortable and uneasy behind the wheel of your car. You are picturing and thinking about all the negatives that could go wrong instead of simply relaxing and driving.

What are the characteristics and attitudes that make a great putter?
Relaxed, focused, and keep it simple. They believe they are a great putter. They don't even need to have a great putting stroke. They just need to believe they are a great putter. I ask my juniors, every day, who is the best putter in the world. They are not answering themselves, so I kid around with them a little bit! I verbally say, "Hey man, you are the quarterback. Who is the quarterback of your team? It better be you. If you are not going to believe in yourself over a putt, if you can't simply get confidence and believe that you are going to knock it in before it goes in, if you think you have to make your stroke technically perfect before it goes in, you are thinking backwards." You need to believe it's going in before you do anything. Keep it simple and relaxed.

> *"Speed skill is absolutely the most important quality to good putting."*

If you had to pick one golfer as a role model for putting, who would it be, why, and what would make them a role model?
There are so many great putters out there, statistically. If you were to go over time, it would have been Loren

Roberts, Ben Crenshaw, Tiger Woods at his height. I have really enjoyed how Rory McIlroy is playing. Dave Stockton and that group have really helped him virtually take very little time over the ball, stand behind it, move in rhythm and really get through the putt very solid, very firm, and very relaxed. Rory was just fantastic in the US Open. If anybody could get a video of how well he putted in the US Open, it was phenomenal.

Putts within 10 feet are the most stressful. How should golfers approach this situation especially to avoid the dreaded 3 putt?
Well, it comes back to speed. From inside 10-feet you are hoping to touch the hole. The true number on tour of statistical data over time for a three-footer is 95% or 98%. A six footer is just about 50% on the PGA Tour. As you get to six feet, if you miss it by a half a ball at three feet, that thing is going in the hole. But another three feet further out, it's lipping out on the edge. So the whole idea with 10 feet, is you still need to control your speed. Speed skill is absolutely the most important quality to good putting. If you miss it a foot to the side but you are on speed, you only have a one footer. How often have you seen people putt a 15 footer and putt it five feet short or five feet long? But how often do you see somebody putt from 15 feet and hit it five-feet to either side? Very seldom. So you might miss it by a foot to the side, but if your speed is dead on the hole, or a foot by, at the most you have a foot putt. So you have to control your speed.

What do you need to do to be a good putter? Are there any tips, techniques, or tricks, that have really helped you, your students, or the pros?
You need a good routine and good practice habits. You need to regularly practice distance control and never hit putts the same length back to back. Always hit different length putts back to back; 3 footers, 6 footers, 9 footers,

12 footers, 15 footers; repeat. Never hit the same distance back to back.

That goes against what you see a lot of people do, set up three balls all at the same distance.
I never want people to do that. I want them to change their distance on each putt so they constantly have to reevaluate how far they need to putt. That's what leads you to be a better 1st-ball putter, and get out of a bad practice habit, gauge it on the first one and then fix it on the second or third. You need to be a better 1st-ball putter in the game.

A low score in golf depends on a variety of clubs, skills, and shots. What do you recommend to balance putting in conjunction with these other demands during a round of golf, such as after good shots, after bad shots, or being in a rut?
Bad shots are what happens if they don't have proper routines. They are not taking deep breaths, and they are not learning to bring their concentration point to a much more relaxed state where they can quiet their mind. Have a very clear focal point and learn to relax and quiet your mind and make the stroke.

What are the realistic expectations of putts per hole or putts per round or other measures that golfers need to follow as they develop their skills?
They average 2 putts per hole, so they should be around 36 putts max. For every 3 putt, you want to have a 1 putt that makes up for that 3 putt. The whole idea is you want to be less than 2 putts. 36 putts for a pro and they want to kill themselves. That's a huge number for them. I just asked a student today, "How many times do you 3 putt?" He shoots high 90's and low 100's and all he wanted to do was work on his driver. I asked him about the 3 putting and he said, "Seven, eight, or nine times a round." And I

said "You've got to let me work on your putting sometime soon." "Okay!", but he wanted to work on the driver.

That is what I have observed: people want to go to the sizzle of the driver, but they don't use that nearly as often as they do the putter.
A lot of times, if you ask somebody straight up, they don't care about putting. They don't care about shooting that lowest score. They want to hit that ball over 200 yards in the air and hit it somewhat straight. So if you ask somebody honestly, "Would it be okay if you hit it 175 yards down the middle of the fairway every time and learned how to putt really well and shoot a good score? Or is it really important to you to hit your drives longer and straighter?" Most people will say, "I want to hit it harder and farther." They don't want to suck off the tee as bad. They come back and complain about their score, but they really need to reevaluate what that commitment is. If you ask them honestly, more than 50-70% of the people are going to say they want to hit it farther.

Looking back, is there anything about putting and golf you wish you had done differently? What do you know now that you wish you had known sooner?
I wish I would have understood how to read greens by AimPoint, that is basically reading it with your feet and knowing where the high and the low points are without trusting your eyes. I am teaching beginners to learn to putt faster by understanding certain technologies that are out there and I am using AimPoint. Some of the stuff they are coming up with is just flat out amazing to understand how a ball rolls on a green.

What are your most humbling and most memorable putts?
I have 5 putted a green before in a tournament, which is pretty humbling, and I have made a double or triple break putt before I got over it and just thought, "This is an

impossible putt," but I relaxed and made the stroke and it went in.

What would you hope golfers would take away from this interview?
I would like people to learn to putt more like a six year old. There's a club, a ball, and a hole, and you simply need to aim the putter face somewhere along the line that the ball needs to roll. You need to really un-clutter your mind to putt as if you were a six-year-old, and keep it that simple. A six-year-old is not going to build a very technical, conceptual idea about putting; they are going to aim that putter, draw it back, and hit it towards the hole. They are completely stoked and excited when the putt goes in and then stoked and excited to hit the next putt whether or not they missed it or made it. So watching enough kids putt and watching adults putt, adults need to put more like a child.

Is there anything else you want to share? Anything that I haven't asked that I should be asking?
Again, I think you need to be the star of your movie, the quarterback of your team, the person on the free throw line at the end of the game that feels like they can make both free throws to win. You need to exercise your confidence and your mind and will the ball to go in. It's so important. Do you start making putts and therefore become more confident, or do you start making more putts because you are more confident? They are definitely intertwined, but I believe that negative talk, negative imagery, things like that need to be cleaned up. The simple fact is: when you putt, it is simply going to go in or not, and to be afraid of the outcome of it going in is inhibiting. So I believe you need to learn how to relax, make a good putt, and detach from it. You can't control it once it is off your putter. The whole idea is you need to find a way to putt like that child—simply aim the putter face, pull it back, hit it, and let go.

I applaud your concept; it's right on. If people are really upset about being a 25-36 handicap, let's go watch them putt. That's the fastest area in the game to save five shots a round. That's where people can make the quickest improvement.

Remember driving, pitching, and putting are the three most important aspects of the game. So when people say, "Drive for show, putt for dough." The best total driver on tour, meaning statistically combined with the length and accuracy, made more money than the best total putter on the tour. So the longest hitter that hit the most fairways combined, made more money. It just so happens that those guys are not bad putters either.

> *"That's the fastest area in the game to save five shots a round."*

Mike Shannon

One of America's Top 50 Greatest Teachers (Golf Digest)

"Every player has the ability to putt as well as the best putters on tour."

Mike is a PGA Class A professional and he brings years of experience to the Sea Island Golf Learning Center. Mike teaches at the Sea Island Golf Academy and has worked with over 100 PGA, LPGA, Champions Tour, and Nationwide Tour players. Mike served as director of golf at Old Waverly Golf Club, Montgomery Country Club, and Isleworth Country Club prior to joining Sea Island in 2003. A short game expert, Shannon invented the Laser Optics Putting Improvement System that is currently used by more than 100 tour players. Mike has made numerous television appearances, including an appearance on the Golf Channel's "Golf Academy Live."

His current students include U.S. Open champion Lucas Glover, 2009 Masters champion Angel Cabrera, 5 Time PGA Tour winner Jonathan Byrd, Ryder Cup captain Davis Love III, 2009 two-time tour winner Brian Gay, Milwaukee Open winner Bo Van Pelt, Charles Howe, Vijay Singh, Alice Miller, Charles Warren, Davis Love, Ian

Leggatt, Shaun Micheel, Tadd Fujikawa, Steve Lowery, Tom Kite, John Harris, Jay Sigel, Graham Marsh, Joe Durant, Heath Slocum, Paula Creamer, and Jan Stephenson.

- Golf Digest's list of "America's 50 Top Greatest Teachers" 2009
- Golf Magazine's "Top 100 Greatest Teachers" 2011
- Innovative Teacher of the Year, Golf Magazine, 2008
- Top Teacher, Golf Digest, 2000-2008
- Top Teacher, Golf Magazine, 2000-2008
- PGA Teacher of the Year, Gulf States Section, 1992, 1994 Dixie Section 2001

There are millions of new and high handicapped golfers playing every year. How do these golfers need to view the importance of putting in their game?
Well the first thing they have to realize is 40% of all the shots they take on the golf course are going to be with their putter. They use their putter twice as much as they use any other club in their golf bag.

The putt can be the most important, most frustrating, and most misunderstood and least practiced shot in golf. What are the key things about the putt that every golfer needs to fully understand to build a base for accurate, consistent, and enjoyable putting?
Every player has the ability to putt as well as the best putters on tour. There are no physical limitations to being a great putter. You don't have to be big, you don't have to be strong, and you don't have to flexible like you do when you are developing your full swing. The only thing is, if you are going to be a great putter, you have to do what

> *"Every player has the ability to putt as well as the best putters on tour."*

great putters do and that is what I have spent 17 years researching. So there are commonalities to being a great putter.

Can you share some of those?
Everybody has a ball position, a front to back ball position, which matches with their vision and dominant eye to create a perfect aim. It's not the same with everybody so there is no one ball position for every player. Every one of us has a spot somewhere along the front to back line that if the ball is there we are going to aim perfectly. If the ball gets in front of that spot, we are going to aim left; if it gets behind that spot we are going to aim to the right. Now the importance of that line is if your ball is out of position by one inch, it can change your aim by three inches for every 10 feet. Second thing is that the natural putting stroke has a slight arc to it. The reason it does is because the shaft of the address is an incline plane; it's not a vertical plane. Because of that, the natural shape of the putting stroke is going to be that of an arc. The only way that the putter can naturally work straight back and straight forward is if the shaft is vertical at address, which is actually against the rules of golf. So since we have an inclined plane, the natural motion of the putter is that of an arc. Since it is an arc, if your putter face stays square to that natural arch it will open 4 degrees at 6 inches back and it would close 4 degrees at 6 inches forward of impact.

> *"...if you are going to be a great putter, you have to do what great putters do..."*

So, 8 degrees total face rotation is mathematically a perfect putting stroke. However, on the tour we see a range between 6-12 degrees. For instance, a player like Loren Roberts, David Toms, Mike Weir, and Matt Kuchar — they are all 3 degrees open and 3 degrees close. So they have 6 degrees total rotation in their putting stroke.

Now, Jim Furyk, V.J. Singh, Tiger Woods, Davis Love, Zach Johnson—they are all 6 degrees open and 6 degrees close, so they have a 12 degree rotation in their putting stroke. The reason that is important is because the average collegiate player that we see at Sea Island has a total face rotation between 24 and 28 degrees. When you have that much rotation in your putting stroke, the squareness of your putter depends solely upon timing and impact, which of course under pressure timing tends to disappear. So the most successful putters on the tour have eliminated that timing factor by reducing the amount of face rotation in their putting stroke.

The second thing is that good putters all get into a very similar setup position. When we talk about that, at address, the shaft of the putter is an extension of the forearms. The shaft of the putter runs neither underneath the arms, nor above the arms at address. The right arm angle from the tip of the shoulder to the middle of the arm at the elbow to the finger tips, should be less than 135 degrees. Anytime the arm angle gets longer or straighter than 135 degrees two things tend to happen. First, the rotation of the putter starts to increase. Secondly, is the consistency of the path of the putter starts to decrease. What I see in a lot of players is them standing too tall, which puts their arms too long, which in turn creates more rotation and more inconsistency in the stroke.

Now the next thing is at address, the spine angle from the back of the neck to the belt to the back of the shoe should be between 113 and 123 degrees. It's not unusual for the average amateur to stand 132 or 133 degrees of spine angle, so they are standing too tall at address. Again, that lengthens the arms, which in turn creates a lot of inconsistencies in the stroke.

So, these little things that we look for being face rotation and consistency of path is a result of a proper setup position.

A proper setup position has a spine angle between 113 and 123 degrees with the right arm angled under 135 degrees.

You hear about golfers throwing and breaking putters over missed putts. What are the biggest mistakes you see golfers make that limit their putting ability?
It's lack of getting prepared to hit the putt by not really analyzing what they are facing with the putt. Being the distance of the putt, whether it is uphill or downhill, how much break the putt has in it, what speed they are going to hit the putt, and because of this they hit putts that are not successful. As a result your frustration tends to set in.

In your experience, what are the road blocks that prevent golfers from becoming good putters?
Improper information. To preface that, putting has changed so much over the last 60 years. Prior to 1965, because of the conditions of the putting surfaces, the putting stroke was really nothing more than just a flick of the wrist. Bobby Jones, Gene Sarazen, Ben Hogan, Sam Snead, Byron Nelson, Arnold Palmer and Billy Casper — all of their putting strokes had a tremendous amount of wrist in the stroke because they needed to get the ball up on top of the grass so it would roll. Now, by 1965 the conditions of the putting surfaces had become such that the best putters on tour had started to eliminate that excess motion. They started to use bigger muscles — the arms — and the putting stroke became more of an arms-back and arms-forward type of motion. Now in 1996, we started to see a new putting stroke come to the tour and it was a putting stroke brought to the tour by these young players who had actually grown up on better putting surfaces. The putting stroke that these players brought to the tour involved even bigger muscles of the body, being the upper back, shoulders, and chest. So what these young players did is they just locked into a position and the putting stroke was nothing more than just the movement of these big muscles. Now, we have to look at what period did the instructor learn

how to putt? If the instructor learned how to putt prior to 1965, they are probably going to teach a little bit more of a hand type of stroke; if they learned to play between 1965 and 1996 you are probably going to see more of an arm type of stroke, when in fact we know that both of those strokes are obsolete for today's putting surfaces.

Every weekend we see professionals miss simple putts. Why? What is going on that makes them miss these seemingly easy putts?
That's a great question and I have posed the same question to our sports psychologist that we have on staff here. Pretty much what you get is a lack of focus. They have just consented to the fact that they are going to walk up and just tap this putt in when in fact there are some factors that they didn't see. Whether it's more break or less break, or uphill or downhill, or they just really didn't get ready to make their best stroke. As a result, they have missed that easy putt.

What are the characteristics and attitudes that make a great putter?
The great putters try to make putts. Mediocre and poor putters try not to 3 putt. When we were all young we were great putters because we expected to make those putts. We went out there and we tried to make those putts. We didn't care if we 3 putted; we just tried to make the putts. But as we got older, then we got into a position where we knew the 3 putt could hurt us. So we turned from an offensive-type of putting game into a defensive-type of putting game. As a result, we just don't make as many putts as we should.

> *"The great putters try to make putts."*

If you had to pick one golfer as a role model for putting, who would it be, why, and what would make them a good role model?

Now, the question was not who has the best stroke or who is the best putter, because that doesn't always go hand in hand. If we are talking about who I would like to model my putting stroke after, it would be David Toms. David probably has, mechanically, as good if not the best putting stroke out there. If you are talking about making a putt, then definitely Brandt Snedeker. If you have ever been around Brant you know he is not thinking about a 3 putt. He is going to try to make every putt he looks at and I tell you, with that attitude right there, that's the reason he leads the PGA Tour in putting.

Putts within 10 feet are the most stressful. How should golfers approach this situation especially to avoid the dreaded 3 putt?
Good question. First off, the reason they are most stressful is because those are the putts, to us, that we should make. If we are out 20-30 feet, and we hit a putt that does not go in but finishes close to the hole, we are very satisfied with that. Once we get inside 10 feet our success is measured by how many of those putts go into the hole. So, we have to narrow everything. We have to narrow our aim, we have to be more specific with our read and we have to be more specific with the speed of the putt. So players get into that 10-feet area

> *"You want to get up there and make the best stroke you can."*

and they are trying to guide the ball into the cup instead of just making a stroke that they have made to get to that point. Again, that's just changing the attitude. You want to get up there and make the best stroke you can. You can't guide a putt into the hole. There are only a few things you can do and not all good putts go into the cup. All you can do is to stand up there, be prepared, and then make as good of a quality stroke as you possibly can.

What do you need to do to be a good putter? Are there any tips, techniques, or tricks, that have really helped you, your students, or the pros?
The first thing is the ability to aim the putter. Bottom line in putting, if you can't aim the putter you can't putt. Every stroke has to be a manipulated motion and it's so important that a player learn how to aim the putter correctly. That is a product of the front to back ball position; it's determined by the vision and dominant eye of the player. So number one, first and foremost, you give me a player who can aim the putter and I will show you a guy who can make some putts.

> *"Bottom line in putting, if you can't aim the putter you can't putt."*

A low score in golf depends on a variety of clubs, skills, and shots. What do you recommend to balance putting in conjunction with these other demands during a round of golf, particularly after good shots, bad shots, or being in a rut?
Well, the tie-in between all of the shots, whether it's the tee shot or the approach shot or a good recovery shot from off the green and the putt, all rely on consistent tempo and rhythm. You have to maintain this tempo and rhythm in every shot that you hit. You can't have a tempo and rhythm with your tee shot and have a different tempo and rhythm with your approach shot, and yet another different tempo and rhythm with your putting stroke. They all have to match. That's why the tour players are so good because they can hold that consistent tempo and rhythm from the first tee to the last green. Now, the rest of us, we can get it going for two or three holes at a time, but then it tends to leave us. Then it will come back and then it will leave us again and that's how we shoot what we do.

You look at the players that we have considered to have beautiful swing—players who come to mind would be

Payne Stewart, Tom Purtzer, Al Geiberger. What really tied those three together was not the mechanics, because literally they didn't have the best of mechanics, but they really had beautiful tempo and beautiful rhythm.

I have noticed that when you have a really good tempo and rhythm and you are not forcing it is when you have the best shots.
That might be the biggest lesson in golf right there.

What are the realistic expectations of putts per hole, putts per round, or other measures that golfers need to follow as they develop their skills?
Number one, we are looking for putts per round to be under 30. Putts per green hit in regulation, which for a beginner is not going to be a big deal, but for a more advanced player it should be at least under 1.80. At one point this year, the top 100 putters on the PGA Tour were separated by 1/8th (.125) of a putting stroke per round.

Looking back is there anything in putting and golf you wish you had done differently? What do you know now that you wish you had known sooner?
Everything. It's amazing how as we get older our eyes are open to different things. I have done so much research into putting over the last 17 years, and when I was a young player and a collegiate player—I played a little bit on the tour—and I was not aware of these things. Like everybody else I struggled to get the ball into the cup and if I had just known what I know today, I think it would have been a different story.

> *"...they can hold that consistent tempo and rhythm from the first tee to the last green."*

What are your most humbling and most memorable putts?

Humbling would be when I was playing in an old Hogan Tour event. In front of about 2,000 spectators on the last hole I had hit a putt up to about 6 inches, walked up to tap it in and completely missed the cup with it.

The most memorable would have been in the Deposit Guarantee Classic. The Deposit Guarantee used to be the tour opposite the Masters. I had hit my approach shot to maybe one foot onto the putting surface. The pin was as far back on the putting green as you could possibly get. It had to have been at least 120 feet. I still remember seeing that putt break three different directions and go into the cup. I liked that one!

What do you hope golfers take away from this interview?
What I hope they take away is that they can be as good a putter as anybody on the tour. All they have to do is do what good putters do. If they will spend their time working in that direction, then they will see a lot of putts on the golf course go into the cup.

Is there anything else you would like to share? Anything you think that may help fellow golfers?
Well, the one thing that players do is when they get ready to buy a putter, they walk into the golf shop, look at the current popular models, and just pick one and go. When in fact the design of the putter can help or hurt them, in my opinion, up to 1 or $1^{1/2}$ strokes per round. Some players need offset in their putter, some players need non-offset, some players need toe weight, some need face balance, some players need longer putters, some players need shorter putters, some players need heavier putters, and some players need lighter putters. All of these things go in to helping that player become better with their putting game.

> *"...they can be as good a putter as anybody on the tour."*

Andy Thompson
Golf Digest Top 100 Fitter

"Green guessing to green reading is a huge step for people."

Andy has been teaching golf for seven years and averages over 100 students per year. He is a Golf Digest Top 100 Fitter, a certified AimPoint Green-Reading Instructor, and an Edel Putter Fitter.

Andy is the primary club-fitter at Totally Driven and has worked with numerous tour professionals, and club professionals. He has worked with top amateurs as well as beginners to insure each player has properly fit equipment using state of the art technologies.

He is a Putting Zone Certified Instructor, AimPoint Certified Instructor and SAM PUTT Instructor. Having studied under Geoff Mangum, David Edel, Mark Sweeney, David Orr, and others, he is well versed in putter fitting and instruction.

www.totallydriven.com

There are millions of new and high handicapped golfers playing every year. How do these golfers need to view the importance of putting in their game?
Well, putting is 40-45% of the strokes incurred in a game of golf, so if you don't put that level of attention to it, your results are going to be sub-standard. What you see out there typically is people banging away with the driver at the driving range and you are only hitting maybe 14 drives on a round of golf. As far as putting, you are putting about 35 times, for the average golfer. There's a huge discrepancy in the amount of time spent on putting verses the driver or hitting irons or the shots, that really don't come into play as often as the putter does.

The putt can be the most important, most frustrating, and most misunderstood and least practiced shot in golf. What are the key things about the putt that every golfer needs to fully understand to build a base for accurate, consistent, and enjoyable putting?
The emphasis are the four main facets of putting, and I don't think people understand this. How you aim your putter, the ability to control your distance, green reading, and then the stroke. The putting stroke itself is going to be influenced by the other three elements, so in other words, if you aim your putter left, your stroke is going to be such that you are going to manipulate your face open to be able to hit the putt more on target. If your distance is poor, your stroke is going to reflect that, and if you're green reading is consistently off, your stroke is going to be inconsistent. These are really the four main elements and a lot of times people get hooked on working on the stroke, which is arguably, fourth in the hierarchy. Aim, distance control, and green reading are probably a little more important than the stroke because the stroke is

> *"There's a huge discrepancy in the amount of time spent on putting verses the driver..."*

more of an intuitive thing, and if you are doing the other three things incorrectly or not very well, your stroke is going to ride along with them.

You hear about golfers throwing or breaking their putters over missed putts. What are the biggest mistakes you see golfers make that limit their putting ability?
The biggest thing is not really understanding green reading and how the putt is going to break; uphill, downhill, and the influences of the green itself. The other one would be the perception that you should make every six-foot putt. The PGA Tour average on a five or six-foot putt is not nearly as high (~50%) as what people think. I think sometimes you get a false impression by watching TV because the players on the tour that are seen on TV are really the players that are doing well that particular round.

> *"...the average player is not very good at green reading..."*

In your experience, what are the road blocks that prevent golfers from becoming good putters?
That's one of them right there—too high of expectations. Another one would be that they aren't good green readers. When we do green reading classes and I have eight people going through a session, I will have all eight people stand below the hole and drop a ball on where they think a straight uphill putt is. The average space between the person on the right and the person on the left from 15 feet away from the hole is going to be about 15-20 feet. So the average player is not very good at green reading, they don't understand green reading and they don't think they need to learn green reading.

Typically, how long does it take someone to learn that?
Well, we do it in two half-hour sessions. Now, that doesn't teach them everything they need to know, but that gives

them a good starting point. From there, they will start to understand green shapes. They are going to understand the rules of physics and math as to why putts break the way that they break, and start understanding the different elements of green reading that are needed, rather than what they have been using in the past, which is not much more than green guessing.

So, going from green guessing to green reading?
Yes, green guessing to green reading is a huge step for people and it's hardly ever been taught throughout the history of golf. So this is an area that is really untapped.

Every weekend we see professionals miss simple putts. Why? What is going on that makes them miss these seemingly easy putts?
Well, first of all the green conditions on the tour is quite a bit more severe than the courses we are playing on. The green speeds are much faster, the margin for error is much smaller, and there are subtle breaks. There are a lot of things that would go into a good player missing a putt and it comes down to really the four things that I mentioned before. They may have an aim issue or if they didn't control their distance correctly that is going to influence how much the putt is going to break. Green reading, again, is a huge factor. It's amazing now that I have worked with Mark Sweeney, AimPoint founder, and understand green reading better. When I watch television I get a whole different perception on how well these guys are reading greens. I can see them in a spot, where the read should be fairly simple (even on TV where it's difficult to tell if they have a putt that breaks a certain way) and they are totally misreading it. A simple putt is getting misread more than you would think.

> *"...green guessing to green reading is a huge step for people..."*

The stroke is obviously a factor, but when you get to the level of a professional, it's probably even less of a factor because those guys and gals have strokes that are grooved. They are working on it, they have a repeating stroke, and it's probably appropriate for how they aim their putter. So it probably comes down most often to green reading and human error.

What are the attitudes and characteristics that make a great putter?
I would say a positive and confident attitude. Of course, if you don't practice the right things and work on the right things it's hard to develop a positive and confident attitude. You need to have success to feel confident, and it's hard to be positive if you don't have success. Part of this is understanding putting a little bit better and working on the right things to develop a whole persona of, "I am going to make this putt," rather than the self-destructive sense that people have right now where they are thinking they are not going to make the putt or are not sure of how hard to hit the putt or where to aim the putt or how much it is going to break. You really need to have control over how far you are going to hit your putt, understanding that you are aiming your putter where you believe you are aiming your putter, and a good process for green reading so that you are confident that you are going to be aiming at the right point and the putt is going to break as much as you believe it is going to break. If you don't have those things, it's really hard to develop the positive attitude and the confidence that you need to become better.

> *"You really need to have control over how far you are going to hit your putt..."*

If you had to pick one golfer as a role model for putting, who would it be and what would make them a good role model?
It would be hard to pick one. Luke Donald is obviously one that you would pick and he has an excellent short game. He focuses on his short game and he is up high in the putting stats. He doesn't hit the ball real far, yet is the number one ranked golfer in the world because he can get the ball in the hole. He spends the appropriate amount of time on his short game because he realizes that is his bread and butter. Now, I don't believe Luke is AimPoint trained, so I believe he could become even better. Obviously, at his level he is a very good green reader, but I think he could become even better.

Putts within 10 feet are often the most stressful. How should golfers approach this situation, especially to avoid the dreaded 3 putt?
First of all, 3 putting from within 10 feet shouldn't happen too often. The reality is you should be getting the ball up around the hole, within 6-12 inches of the hole, from 10 feet. With the right techniques—the ability to aim your putter, control your distance, read the green correctly—you really shouldn't be 3 putting from that area. If we talk about not making the putt from 10 feet, a lot of times that is just expectations being too high and expecting to make every 10-foot putt or every eight-foot putt, is really unrealistic. Players need a better understanding of what the real expectation is, and on Mark Sweeney's website, www.aimpointgolf.com, there is some good information on the putting percentages. If people understood that, they would not put as much pressure on themselves, expecting to make every 10-foot putt, which is not doing them any good. The frustration that comes with not making the putt is a detriment to their golf game.

What do you need to do to be a good putter? Are there any tips, techniques, or tricks, that have really helped

you, your students, or the pros?
I can tell you the things I see most often, which is the head moving and not being steady overall, number one. Number two is timing; timing of the stroke is not taught a lot, but I think it is very, very important. Geoff Mangum taught me a lot about this and he is really one of the putting gurus. Timing of the stroke and not going from fast to slow or slow to fast, not decelerating into it or hitting at the putt is very important. Another one is too much rotation or too much wrist involved in the putting stroke, especially near the golf ball, near the impact of the stroke.

> *"...90% of players that come into our shop cannot aim their putter over the hole from 6-feet away."*

Then the last one is really a stroke that is based on poor aim, which is going to be a hard stroke to be effective. I see this all the time because 90% of players that come into our shop cannot aim their putter over the hole from 6-feet away. We will aim test them with a laser and a mirror on the putter face and it's amazing how far people can be off from six feet. It's probably about 40% of people, that far off from six feet, believe it or not. If you are that far off from six feet, just think of the manipulation that you need to do to make the ball go right. So if you are aiming left 10 inches, you have to have some type of manipulation of 10 inches from six feet to get the ball to go straight.

A low score in golf depends on a variety of clubs, skills, and shots. What do you recommend to balance putting in conjunction with these other demands during a round of golf, such as after good shots, bad shots, or being in a rut?
When it comes down to it, it's really one shot at a time. The only important shot is the next shot you are going to be taking and having the appropriate amount of focus on

that next shot. So the player needs to really let go of any previous shots or any subsequent shots that are going to be coming up or holes that are going to be played later in the round, and really have the appropriate amount of focus on the very next shot. When it comes to putting, focus needs to be applied before you When it comes to putting even get on the putting green. When effective green reading is put into play, you need to be able to start getting an understanding of the shape of the green and what type of putt you are going to have before you even get on the green.

So the focus gets applied, often, way too late in putting. It's after everybody has read their putt and now the player is taking 10-20 seconds to read their putt when in reality they should have already had a pretty good understanding as to what that putt was going to do from the fairway, four or five minutes ago. Once on the green it's more affirmation of what you saw walking up to the green.

What are the realistic expectations of putts per hole, putts per round, or other measures that golfers need to follow as they develop their skills?
Well, what I would call 'good' would be 30 putts or less per round, and limiting 3 putts to one or less per round. Neither of those would be called great because you would see the players on the PGA Tour are playing under more difficult green situations than what the average player is playing, and they still average less putts per round than that. They are very disappointed when they 3 putt, but for the average player that would be a good starting point. Quite honestly, it's a goal that anybody should be able to get to, if

> *"When it comes to putting, focus needs to be applied before you When it comes to putting even get on the putting green."*

they practice the right things, get the right instruction, and work on it diligently. But very few people are really hitting those numbers right now.

Looking back, is there anything about putting and golf you wish you had done differently? What do you know now that you wish you had known sooner?
The green reading was probably the biggest 'Aha!' for me, followed by AimPoint. Those two elements are so important. I didn't learn about them until the last six or seven years. I have been playing golf a long time, but didn't understand that I wasn't aiming my putter very well and I quite frankly wasn't a very good green reader. I thought I was a pretty good green reader until I got trained by Mark Sweeney and fully understood the nuances. So, if I were to learn anything at an earlier age it would be those two things: getting a putter in my hand that is fit to me so I can aim where I think I am aiming it, and the ability to read greens. Those two elements really stick out for me.

> *"The green reading was probably the biggest 'Aha!' for me..."*

What are your most humbling and most memorable putts?
I know I have had a number of 4 putts in my life, which are always very humbling. I have missed putts within a foot before. I do remember one particular putt where I had an incredibly fast downhill putt on a slope of about 5% grade. The green was so fast it was actually cracked; it was drying out in the heat, it was very hot out and the green was getting burnt as play was going on. I hit a putt downhill that probably would have gone about an inch. The putt actually stopped three times before it got to the hole and it kept trickling on and ended up right in the middle of the hole from about 15-20 feet away. That one was

pretty memorable.

What do you hope golfers take away from this interview?
Well, first of all that there is hope out there and anybody can become a better putter. Secondly, that there are some technologies out there and resources that can help them, fit them with the right putter, and be able to read greens better than what they are doing right now. It's really the education, that there is some improvement out there that maybe isn't too well known that could help them improve their putting.

Is there anything else you would like to share? Anything you think may help that I have left out?
Everything should actually start with the fitting. Basically, most players select a putter off the rack with no idea if they're aiming it correctly, controlling their distance correctly, have the right loft and lie angles, the right length, or if they need a face-balance putter or toe-hang putter, and they are getting into the wrong equipment right away. We have a process called the Edel Golf Fitting System, where we fit players, based on how they are aiming their putter, their ability to control distance, obviously getting them into the right loft/lie and length of the putter. Having a putter in their hand where they can aim where they think they are aiming it and being able to control their distance by having a putter that is properly weighted, balanced, and swing-weighted for them is much more important than what people think.

> *"...anybody can become a better putter."*

Mardell Wilkins
Top 50 Best Teacher, Golf Digest and LPGA

"Great putters; that's something they all have: rhythm and good feel."

Mardell Wilkins has been teaching golf for 27 years and averages 300-400 students per year.

- LPGA Top 50 Best Teacher 2008 – 2009 Golf Digest Top 50 Best Teachers in America 2010-2011
- Golf for Women Top 50 Teachers 2000
- Two time LPGA Teacher of the Year, Western Section

There are millions of new and high handicap golfers playing every year; how do you feel these golfers need to view the importance of putting in their game?
For most beginners, the main thing they are interested in at first is just to hit the ball so they can get on the course. But, if you start them on a putting green close to the hole and get them used to the idea of some success by putting the ball in the hole, then let them understand that a one-foot putt is going to count as much as the 200 yard

drive, most will likely never hit in their life. Bottom line of golf is the lowest score and if you can't putt you can't have a low score.

The putt can be the most important, most frustrating, and most misunderstood and least practiced shot in golf. What are the key things about the putt golfers need to fully understand to build a base for accurate, consistent, and enjoyable putting?
They need to understand the basics and mechanics of the stroke. There are obviously schools of opinion whether it's straight back, straight through, or an arc, but I am always teaching a straight back, straight through, and the importance of the putt stance that we call square to the path. I usually start them out with some drills to help visualize that.

You hear about golfers throwing or breaking putters over missed putts, particularly the dreaded 3 putt. What are the biggest mistakes you see golfers make that limit their putting ability?
Tension is number one, caring too much about making the putt rather than making a good stroke. I had a putting lesson from Manuel De Latorre. The De Latorre family has been teaching golf in this country for a very, very long time. When I was on tour, and played one of his students, what impressed me was how beautifully they would roll the ball on the green. One thing he said always stuck in my brain; he said, "Mardell, I never try to make a putt. I read the green, give it the best read I can, and adjust speed and make the best stroke I can. I can't control whether the ball goes in or not." I thought about that a lot and realized it's true because the reason I got iffy is because I cared too

> *"Bottom line of golf is the lowest score and if you can't putt you can't have a low score."*

much whether the ball was going in the hole or not. He really changed my mindset after that.

In your experience, what are the road blocks that prevent golfers from becoming better putters?
Certainly lack of patience is one of them. A lot of people think you are born a good putter, but that's not true. Putters spend a gazillion hours practicing their mechanics to the point where they can learn to forget their mechanics and just work on their feel when putting. That's where it has to get to. Too many golfers are always working on their mechanics on the course and it takes away from rhythm and feel. Great putters; that's something they all have: rhythm and good feel.

Every weekend we see professionals miss simple putts. Why? What is going on that makes them miss these seemingly easy putts?
I would disagree that those putts are always easy. When they are playing under certain conditions, those greens are so speedy and they don't pick golf courses with flat greens, I can promise you that. So for a seemingly easy three-foot putt, you have to have such perfect line and pace. For a player who is aggressive and tends to make the first putt, slightly misjudges the pace or the speed, it's easy to race it four-feet past the hole and then miss the same opportunity coming back. I don't think most people realize how tough the conditions are because the pros can make it look rather easy.

> *"Great putters; that's something they all have: rhythm and good feel."*

What are the characteristics and attitudes that make a great putter?
Obviously they have a lot of confidence. Their mind is very clear in what they intend to do in each situation. You

can see a player, if there is a doubt, call their caddy in for a second opinion, but they clear the clutter before they go ahead and execute. They try to get the doubt out of their minds and think, "I have read this five-foot, downhill, slip putt to break three-inches left to right, and I need to hit it at a dime-in-the-hole kind of speed." They are totally executing.

If you had to pick one golfer as a role model for putting, who would it be, why, and what makes them a good role model?
We could probably answer that one a lot of ways, but I would have to say that it's not going to be Tiger Woods for me. He has a good rhythm, but he's a jam-it-in-the-hole kind of a putter, and I don't think that's a good image for a lot of golfers to have. I can remember a player of my era whom you may know or may not know; her name was Sally Little. She was a great player from South Africa. She had the smoothest putting stroke I have ever seen in my life and I can remember it to this day. Things that you can remember 20 years later, there's something special about them.

> *"...if you can't read the greens you are not going to be a good putter."*

Putts within 10 feet are often the most stressful. How should golfers approach this situation, especially to avoid the dreaded 3 putt?
One thing is setting some realistic expectations. Understanding that those golfers on TV are the best players in the world and usually get shown on TV when they are having the best games of their career. If you look at the stats, players at three feet make most of their puts (95-100%), but when they drop back to eight feet, the overall percentage drops down to about 50%. So don't try put too much pressure on yourself to make your first putt go in,

and instead focus on just making a good putt, and if it goes in great, but if it doesn't, realize you are in that average 50%.

What do you need to do to be a good putter? Are there any tips, techniques, or tricks, that have really helped you, your students, or the pros?
Well, one thing I talked a little bit earlier about is having the good basics. There's a lot of different ways to grip the putter, but the stroke basics of pace and tempo are pretty consistent with good putters. Good putters should always have light hands on the putter, trying to keep the tension out of it. The other thing you have to do to be a good putter is you have to be a good green reader. You have to be able to read line and pace correctly. You can have the best stroke in the world, but if you can't read the greens you are not going to be a good putter.

A low score in golf demands a variety of club skills and shots. What do you recommend to balance putting in conjunction with these other demands during a round of golf after good shots, after bad shots, or being in a rut?
It's interesting, I had to think about that for a second, especially when you talk about the good shots. You see it more on the putting green than anywhere else, but the two best players of our era, Jack Nicklaus and Tiger Woods, when they made a good putt they had a celebration on the green. They were different celebrations, Tiger with his fist pump and his Tiger growl, but Nicklaus, when he would make a significant putt, his putter always went up in the air with his left hand as he walked towards the hole. They were anchoring that memory, they were taking full possession of the positiveness of it.

When you are in a rut you need to change something just for the sake of changing so you are not doing the same thing over and over again and expecting a different result. I don't know if you watched the LPGA this week, but

Michelle Wie had a long putter and she putted brilliantly. She has been struggling with the putter for a while, so that's what she did, she changed something. She has been fiddling with it; she changed grips, changed putters and and this is the first time she went with the long putter. So if you are in a rut, you have to change something.

What are the realistic expectations of putts per hole, putts per round, or other measures that golfers need to follow as they develop their skills?
Putts per hole and round are going to depend a lot on greens in regulations that a golfer does or does not have. If you have somebody who is just a real steady, a consistent ball striker, like one of my female students who has won about 18 club championships. She is a good putter, but I would say her putts per hole is high because she hits a lot of greens in regulation. She's not a long hitter, so she doesn't necessarily have a lot of short putts. She does a lot of 2 putts. If you miss more greens and you have a great short game, you are going to have a lot lower putts per hole. You kind of have to look at your game, to answer that question. But if you are going to miss a lot of greens, you better make sure you have good putts per hole.

Looking back, is there anything about putting or golf you wish you had done differently? What do you know now that you wish you had known sooner?
The whole thing about golf is you have to learn your mechanics, but then you have to learn to forget your mechanics and trust your instinct and your feel. When I was on tour, since I was not putting well, I practiced putting a ton and I was always working on my mechanics. Since I have left that part of my golf life and become a teacher, I see golfers tie themselves up in knots all the time. As a golfer, how many times have you just walked up and casually looked at the putt, not over read it or anything, and you made a great putt. Other times you analyze

it to death and you get yourself all tied up in knots and you stab at it.

What are your most humbling and most memorable putts?
I remember missing a one foot, straight in putt and I didn't even touch the hole one time. That was pretty humiliating.

Too much tension?
Too much fear! Fear of not making it and lack of clear intention that I am just going to make my best stroke and if the ball goes in it goes in. That's one thing I wish I had learned a lot earlier in my career for sure, just to have clear intentions and that I can't control where the ball goes exactly, I can only control what I do as far as tempo and reading my lines and trusting myself.

And what was your most memorable putt?
Since I did have a history of being a sort of yipper when I was on tour, I played in a regional PGA event called TV Team Golf, where teams from one club play a match against teams from another club. It's one male amateur, one female amateur, and one club pro. It's filmed and they show it later on TV. I was the only female pro in the field. We got all the way to the finals and on the last semifinal and final match, I was left with a four-foot putter to win in both matches. Based on my history of yippiness I made both of them, and to me that was my most rewarding. I put those behind me. I was also the only female to ever win it.

> "...there's no magic out there. You have to be willing to work at it..."

What do you hope golfers would take away from this interview?
Well, just that there's no magic out there. You have to be willing to work at it, to practice at it, to get your

fundamentals. It's an ongoing work; it's not, "I've got it and now it's going to be good for the rest of my life." At that point, get back into trying to release the mechanics of it and work on putting. Putting is the artistic part of the game. It's like you're painting a picture and every shot is a little bit different, every stroke of the brush is a little bit different. Honor that.

Is there anything else you would like to share, anything I have left out?
One of the challenges I seem to see a lot, especially with lady club level golfers, is they are too dependent on other people to tell them what to do. They need to learn to take charge of things themselves. In other words, the lady who plays once a week with her husband is always depending on her husband to tell her where to aim and the speed of the putt. I think they need to get beyond that.

Coming back to your question, how many times do people call me up and ask me for a putting lesson? They do, but probably not as frequently as they should. I think more importance should be given to improving your putting.

Sam Emerson
PGA Horton Smith Award Winner for Instructor and Club Fitter

"You can't put the score on the card until you put the ball in the hole."

Sam has been teaching golf for over 50 years and averages 2,000 students per year in group and individual instruction.

- 2003 Minnesota Section PGA Horton Smith Award Winner for Instructor and Club Fitter
- Listed in Guide to America's Top Golf Instructors by the Consumer Research Council of America
- Member of the PGA of America's President's Council for Growth of the Game
- Member of MN Section PGA Education Committee
- Played in US and Senior US Open

www.samemerson.com

There are millions of new and high handicap golfers playing every year. How do these golfers need to view the importance of putting in their game?

The first thing I would say is you can't put the score on the card until you put the ball in the hole. If there are 18 holes, you are going to have to putt at least 18 times.

The putt can be the most important, most frustrating, most misunderstood and least practiced shot in golf. What are the key things about the putt every golfer needs to fully understand to build the base for accurate, consistent, and enjoyable putting?
The number one thing is you have to be able to feel the putter head — the weight of the putter head from swinging it, distance, backwards and forwards. You have to feel it, putting is not mechanical. Great putters are not mechanical putters. They are "feel" putters. One of the best ones I have ever seen is Billy Casper. When I am teaching blind people, which I do a lot of, the only way they can putt is to feel. They cannot see the hole, they have no sense of feel with their shoulders, but they do have sense of feel with their hands.

> *"Great putters are not mechanical putters."*

So to me, the biggest things in putting is to feel the putter head and the distance from the front of your ball to the bowl of the cup. I teach these young people to walk that distance so they know exactly how many steps it is to that cup. They also need to feel the degrees of and the slope with their feet. People with eyes don't do that, they use their eyes instead of their feet to see the slope of the ground. Blind golfers have much better angle of direction than people who see with their eyes. I had a 1 handicapper who was a tremendous putter. That's the biggest thing I have seen about putting.

You hear about golfers throwing or breaking putters over missed putts. What are the biggest mistakes you see golfers make that limit their putting ability?

Moving their bodies. They should be stationary.

Moving their bodies during the putt?
Oh yeah. I see knees moving, I see teeth moving, I see lips moving. It's pretty hard to keep a putter straight if you are moving all your body parts. If you can stand still, put your weight on your left foot, and don't move anything other than your right hand, use your elbow, basically right into your side and that's your base. Your hand is the pendulum of the swing. The hand—if you've ever thrown marbles or thrown a softball, you are using your hand to throw with, back and forth. That's how my blind people putt.

In your experience, what are the road blocks that prevent golfers from becoming good putters?
Too tight a grip—holding that club way too tight. They can't feel enough. If they are doing that, they are also freezing up their bodies when they need to relax. To me, the grip is the most important part of the game. Putting, driving, whatever—you've got to have soft hands and let the club head work. If I have soft hands, that putter is going to go back straight and come back through—it's not going to be moving. If I make a swing with the club, I'm allowing the club to turn on its own, my hands are going to feel that, my hands are going to send the messages to my brain.

> "It's pretty hard to keep a putter straight if you are moving all your body parts."

I hadn't realized most people would grip too hard.
Oh yeah. The only blood you are going to get out of that club is your own, and everybody is trying to get blood out of it, it seems. I had the opportunity to caddy for Sam Snead when I was 15. I asked him very simply, "How tight do you hold the club?" He said, "How tight are you going to hold a baby bird?" I then asked him "If you really want

to hit the ball farther, how hard will you hold the club?" He replied, "Until the club almost falls out of my hand."

Every weekend we see professionals miss simple putts. Why? What is going on that makes them miss these seemingly easy putts?
At that point, it's because they are under pressure. When you are under pressure, how tight do you get? I think they end up getting way too tight, causing them to either go right or left. They are not keeping a square face to the impact of the ball, not when they are tight. I have played a lot of tournaments, but I have never had to play for a million dollars. If I am putting for a million dollars I am going to be relaxed. I am not going to be tight and I know that face is going to be square.

What are the characteristics and attitudes that make a great putter?
From the waist down they are not moving. They are bending and allowing their upper body to do all the work. There's no movement. The eyes are over the ball, they are watching the putter strike the ball. Their attitude is the ball going into the cup, they visualize a coffee can, not the little things that we putt in, and knowing the line of the putt. If you watch them, they are looking at the putt in all directions. The average amateur gets up behind the ball and they don't move, they get behind it and putt to the other side of the cup. As for the blind people, they don't see it, they feel it. They walk from the ball to the hole, get the distance of the putt, and feel what the stroke needs to be.

And you teach all of your students to actually walk the line?
Yes, for pitching, chipping, and putting. You gotta know where the ball is going to land and how far it is from your ball to that hole. When I do it in a group, I ask all 10 of them to stand there, about 20 steps away. Then I ask them

how many steps it would take for them from that spot, and nobody can tell me. People cannot measure distance. But if you walk it, I don't care what your step is, it could be two feet or three feet, but you know how many steps it takes for you to get there. You can do a drill. Go to the side of the green, take one step from the edge, and putt three balls to the edge. Then two steps, three steps, four steps, five steps. You can use this any place on the course. If I have 15 steps, I know it's three multiplied by five, so I am thinking about three times five and back. It's a simple way of measuring distance. That's really what the blind people understand.

> *"If you look at great players, they are feel players."*

There's one thing that is coming out of your method, which is really having people understand a lot more from a "feel" perspective.
Yes. How do you feel playing horseshoes? How do you feel the distance of the stake? When you are bowling, how do you feel that? You know how many feet it is from the line, but how do you feel it? If you look at great players, they are feel players. I have seen some great golfers, Billy Casper being one, he was very soft.

If you had to pick one golfer as a role model for putting, who would it be and why would they make a good role model?
Billy Casper is a perfect one. Ben Crenshaw is as well. I have not found anybody that can make the same movement every time with their shoulders. Tension will create body parts not doing what they usually do, and if you have a different putter, the weight of the putter will change you.

Putts within 10 feet are often the most stressful. How should golfers approach this situation, especially to avoid the dreaded 3 putt?
What I do is I take a deep breath and exhale. I get everything relaxed. I visualize the putt. I have already read the green, and I have walked it. I am putting straight to a point right or left, or it's going to keep going straight. You've got to find that out. I have a 10-foot putt; it's going to break four inches, where do I putt? I putt about a foot and a half in front of that hole and then it's going to break into the hole. I am visualizing that. Great putters, they visualize where the ball is going to go. They visualize the path of the ball.

Do you think a lot of golfers understand the visualization process?
No. I have played in two opens. I visualize how the ball is going to get to the hole. I visualize my swing. What am I doing? What do I want to do? I think about these things. I read an article about a guy that made 2,760 straight shots in basketball, and somebody asked him, "How do you do it?" He said, "I visualize the line from my right hand going into the hoop." That's a pretty good way of doing it with golf too. Visualize where you want the ball to go. I know when I was growing up I heard so many times, "Putt the ball past the hole." I was always visualizing the ball going past the hole and I have never seen a hole behind a hole my whole life. I want it to drop in the hole, so I am visualizing that now.

> *"Great putters, they visualize where the ball is going to go."*

You visualize it dropping into the hole?
Yes, I don't want to visualize it going past. That's the last thing I want.

What do you need to do to be a good putter? Are there any tips, techniques, or tricks, that have really helped you, your students, or the pros?
It took me umpteen years, and I grew up watching great putters. I tell my people, place your putter in the lifeline of your right hand. I want it all the way right, towards the wrist. You take a 10-finger grip; both thumbs down the center of the shaft grip. Make sure your right hand is square to the face. Anchor your right elbow into your right side. You have a little spot, an indentation in your stomach. All you are using is your right hand and forearm to stroke the ball. The left hand follows the right; it does not direct. The left hand holds the club lightly. The right hand is the one that moves the face. 1991 is when I finally found out how to putt. I played at a tournament and I hit 17 greens in regulation. My partner, Jim, he hit five greens in regulation and he was three under. He never made a putt under eight feet—he made everything over. He was the one that showed me about the palms and the hand position. I am a very good putter now.

A low score in golf depends on a variety of clubs, skills, and shots. What do you recommend to balance putting in conjunction with these other demands during a round of golf, such as after good shots, bad shots, or being in a rut?
The biggest thing is still the grip. You can't change because you are upset. You can't be changing that grip. A lot of people miss the shots because they want to try to hit it harder and what they do is tighten up and the club head swings slower. You leave your hand soft and the club head swings back more, it makes release much easier and the ball is going to go farther. I think the biggest part is people hit a bad shot, and then want to make a miracle shot, and it ain't going to happen.

That's what I see. People have a couple bad shots and then they have this mindset of, "Well, I will just birdie

the next two greens and I will be good again," but they haven't birdied any of the holes before that.

Yeah, birdies come when they come; you can't manufacture them. From 150 yards in, is where the score is anyway. I tell people, "Don't look at the pin. Look at something behind the pin and stay within that; you are going to have a small putt."

You can expect miracles to occur on the green, and then it just doesn't happen.

It doesn't. Once in a while something happens, you misread it, but it went in anyway. You better know the local green conditions and breaks, I don't care if it's uphill, downhill, or whatever, it's going that way. That's a local thing. People don't realize some of that stuff.

What are the realistic expectations of putts per hole or putts per round, or other measures that golfers need to follow as they develop their skills?

If you have 1.75 putts per hole that gives you probably 4 shots, 5 shots, as far as putting, that you can save during a round. I was impressed when the guy I played with had 21 putts, par 69. It's not going to happen every day; but for him it might. Think about it; he missed 15 greens and shot 69. Of those five holes, he had 3 birdies for a 21, I had 35.

> "...birdies come when they come; you can't manufacture them."

Looking back, is there anything about putting or golf you wish you had done differently? What do you know now that you wish you had done sooner?

I have improved my putting total—I am a good putter now. Starting to feel that putter head, you just have to allow it to swing.

What are your most humbling or most memorable putts?
Most memorable? I was on the Golf Channel. I made 12 straight, 12-foot putts with a foot and a half break, one handed. My most regretted putt was when I missed my senior tour card by a shot and with a $4^{1/2}$ foot putt.

It's amazing how many things are decided by 1 putt.
Yeah, it is. If I knew then what I know now — that was 1989 — I would have had a totally different feel. I always knew my hands to be soft on a grip as far as hitting a golf ball when I putt.

What do you hope golfers take away from this interview?
They have to be soft, with their hands. You feel what you are doing with your hands, and the putting, its feel. If you are still, you are going to have a good putt. You want to relax. What I hope is that the game should be fun. It's a lot of work, if you want to make it work, but the average player goes out there to have a good time. We hurt ourselves by beating ourselves up. Don't grip the club to get blood out of it.

The other thing is that if you have a problem, go to a PGA professional. That person will teach using just their skills and knowledge. Each client has different needs. This past summer, I was the lead teacher for 10-15 VA people with head injuries. One pro was there and I told him, "This is what we are going to do, we are going to get their feet moving, get their hands soft and the ball in the air." Because their head injuries have some of the same effects as someone with Parkinson's disease, I knew they would be holding the club too tightly. They are starting to lose feeling, they need to get their light feel, it's really that important. One guy couldn't hit the ball 30 feet and by the time he had the ninth and 10th lesson he was really hitting the ball.

> *"Don't grip the club to get blood out of it."*

Is there anything else you would like to share? Anything you think may help your fellow golfers that I left out?
Enjoy the game. It's a game. It's not life or death. If you can get to the plateau of getting on a tour or something, then it's a whole different ball game, but even there I had to be relaxed. To succeed I had to be relaxed and I never got there. I found out early in life that I could miss a shot and still recover. I used my head. If I made the next shot right, I could possibly get in for a third shot, or whatever, then I could make the 1 putt, no miracle shot. That's my philosophy—maintain yourself.

About the Author

Dave was introduced to golf by his parents and began playing at Los Gatos in California. He continued playing in Colorado and participated in numerous golf leagues and groups, as well as many years playing with his parents on the silver and blue courses at the Air Force Academy in Colorado Springs.

After college, Dave worked in engineering and marketing at Hewlett Packard. A senior marketing position supporting the America's Cup and the Volvo golf tour in Europe introduced him to the world of sports marketing.

After leaving HP and a couple other companies, Dave worked as a business consultant and contributed his expertise on golf training aids. He continued this work and a bug was planted to help golfers improve their putting. While in a couple golf leagues, Dave conducted research on golfers, their habits and how they approached putting. Using this valuable information, he worked on improving his putting. While playing golf with his parents at Cougar Canyon in Utah, his mother commented, "your putting has really improved". He was on to something! He continued working on his ideas while visiting the in-laws, Len and Grace, in Myrtle Beach.

After meeting Brian Schwartz, founder of the 50 Interviews series of books, the opportunity arose to work on this book.

The PGA and LPGA professionals Dave approached, supported the book and offered their valuable insights. You hold the results in your hands!

Dave continues to work on other golf projects. Stay tuned!

Acknowledgements

I would like to acknowledge the many people that helped make this book possible:

- My parents who introduced me to the wonderful world of golf
- My wife, Sue, who supports my entrepreneurial efforts
- My in-laws, Len and Grace who introduced me to Myrtle Beach golf
- All the interviewees who provided their valuable insight and time to this project
- Mark Sweeney for his great introduction
- Brian, the founder of 50 Interviews, who has created a system to simplify the publishing process so authors can focus on their writing.

I hope all golfers read this book to better understand themselves and their putting, since we all hate 3 putts!

Dave "No 3 Putts" Perry
no3putts.50interviews.com
dave@50interviews.com | www.no3puttsbook.com

Join the discussions on putting at:

www.facebook.com/no3puttsbook

 @no3puttsbook

Resellers & Affiliates

The internet has made it possible for us to provide our readers a unique opportunity to get paid for referring sales of our books.

Whether you refer the sale for a physical book or an ebook, you can earn a commission of up to 50% of the purchase price.

This is made possible through our affiliate partner, ClickBank. Just register for a free affiliate account at ClickBank and you'll get your own customized URL to use. ClickBank automatically tracks the sale and pays you directly.

To learn more and sign up, visit:
www.50interviews.com/affiliates

CLICKBANK® is a registered trademark of Click Sales, Inc. and used by permission. 50 Interviews Inc. is not an authorized agent or representative of Click Sales, Inc. Click Sales, Inc. has not reviewed, approved or endorsed our books, or any claim, statement or opinion made by 50 Interviews Inc.

CPSIA information can be obtained at www.ICGtesting.com
Printed in the USA
LVOW06s0725100813

347127LV00001B/182/P